Printing Our Way to Poverty

The Consequences of American Inflation

Pat McGeehan

Printing Our Way To Poverty

The Consequences of American Inflation

ISBN 978-0-9857923-0-5

Printed in the U.S.A. by EPP Press

Contents

Part I: Introduction

1. Age of Inflation 5

2. The Fundamentals: Markets vs. Government Planning 13

3. The Analogy 23

4. Basic Origins of Money 29

5. Prosperity under the Gold Standard 35

Part II: Economic Depression

6. Fiat Money and the Business Cycle 45

7. Domestic Boom and Bust: The Plague of the US Economy 51

8. The Keynesian Curse: The Neglect of Savings and Production 63

9. The Market Entrepreneur: A Derivative of Economic Calculation 79

Part III: The Erosion of American Manufacturing

10. Money Creation and the Structure of Production 97

11. The Chinese "Hand Outs" 103

12. Redistribution by the Printing Press: The Heartland to Wall Street and Washington 111

13. Real Income: The Service Sector vs. Manufacturing 117

14. The Inflation Tax and the Myth of Export Stimulus 127

Part IV: Foreign Intervention

15. The Link between Empire and Inflation 135
16. The Follies of British Monetary Coercion 143
17. The Roots of the American "Credit Card" 149
18. The "Production" of Dollars for Reserve Use 155
19. The Fallacy of the War Boom 161

Part V: The Centralization of Power

20. Marx and Keynes: Control of the Money Supply ... 183
21. Social Turmoil 191
22. The Dangers of Centralized Control 203
23. The Coming Bust 211

References

Part I

Introduction

“ …’twas never my desire to trouble the poor with begging.”

-- ***Coriolanus***

Age of Inflation

Nineteenth Century America is often labeled as the Industrial Revolution, the age of Industry. The latter parts of the 20th Century are looked upon as the beginnings of the Information Age, and this term has often characterized the 21st Century as well. In retrospect however, a more appropriate label for this time period is not the Age of Information, but rather the Age of inflation.

Since August 15th, 1971, the infamous date that marked the severance of the final link between the American dollar and gold, the last remnants of the gold standard died and the first international paper standard was given birth. For over forty years now, the world has witnessed unchecked inflation run its course throughout the globalized economy. Over the span of just these few decades, the total American "M2" money supply has grown from a scant 700 billion in 1971, to nearly 10 trillion dollars in 2012—the stock of money increasing by an incredible factor of 14. Very few economists and still fewer politicians have taken the time to understand the repercussions of this money production that has come about from the current fiat, paper dollar standard. In the total absence of sound money policy upon which the nation once thrived, the aim of this book is to shed light on how this Age of Inflation came to be. A multitude of economic and social costs stem from this inflation, some hidden and some not. Thus, this work identifies the consequences wrought by this immense expansion of the money supply, while also explaining the transformation of the American economy under which this "paper standard" has facilitated.

This book targets the largest detrimental results from this government policy of continually increasing the American money supply, all of which are either rooted-in or enabled by this inflation. Government policy of "printing money" has facilitated economic depression, the erosion of the American manufacturing industry, and the growth of US military intervention around the globe. Above all these facilitations though, stands the steady centralization of government power.

Although there are many other symptoms that have come about because of this inflationary epidemic, a sizeable portion of the public is unaware that these experiences are made possible first and foremost by inflation. Hence, widespread education about this root cause is an important hurdle to overcome. A firm grasp is critical if more of the public is to "wrap their arms around" this deep-seated dilemma—as today, inflation has emerged as the most significant calamity our nation's citizens must face in the future economic and political world.

Since the financial collapse in 2008, there seems to be a growing question about the unstable nature of the American economy. In recent years, this is especially true: many Americans are wondering what happened, what causes these financial disasters, and why so many go unemployed. Still more people are concerned about other financial matters, such as the nation's growing national debt, the rising cost of living, and the numerous conflicts being waged and fought by the US military around the globe. Americans today find their relatives frequently overseas in various combat zones, while at home, their paychecks are continually stretched thin, as prices for everyday items such as food, rent, energy, and gasoline persistently eat up their income.

Other facets of life have drastically changed as well. The present standard for a family of four is two bread winners. The norm now is that both parents work; both parents must provide. This is often not by choice, as for many American families it is simply *required.* And it is not just that both parents must work to provide, it is also a question of where they work—or how they provide. Today, it is typical for the average American to work at a bank, or a law firm. Perhaps a doctor's office, or a hospital, or an accounting practice, a shopping outlet, a cell phone distributor, or a retail store.

Presently, the American middle class is defined by the service sector, and it is indeed an infrequent occasion to find a parent who is still employed by industry—or more appropriately defined—the *capital goods* industry. Instead, the vast majority of Americans are now employed by the *consumer goods* sector, or "the service sector". At the heart of this enormous service sector economy of consumption stands the financial services industry—a leviathan of banking conglomerates and Wall Street clearing houses built upon credit. The explosion over the years, the sheer magnitude and size of this financial industry, is difficult to mentally absorb. Over a third of all annual corporate profits in the US economy now come from banking. In 2010, the figure stood around 40%. Compared to just two decades ago, when the American financial sector accounted for less than 20% of profits, this expansion of the heart of the service sector has escalated at a staggering pace.

To the insider, this drift towards banking and services is praised as America's movement away from sweat and toil; the modern making of white collar office work, marked by years of college attendance, made convenient by government direction. But from a more outside point of view, this trend is not of natural occurrence. Fueled by an ever-expanding supply of fiat currency, or money commanded to be so, all of these banking monoliths are the slow but steady product of government. The control of the money supply, the central planning of interest, and above-all, the whims of the central bank, have not only led to a decline in productivity, but have created inconceivable harm to long term American prosperity.

Created by laws of men, the Federal Reserve is the artificial core, and its "funny money" mechanisms are not born of a market economy. In spite of pop economic culture, this massive machine of counterfeit has displaced private productive energies and misaligned the economic structure, giving way to irreparable injury. Today, the new American economic structure is purely rooted on ever-more consumption, a raw fact of life that is quite simply unsustainable.

As mentioned, a closer look will reveal that this growth of financial "service" is only sustainable so long as the supply of paper dollars continues to swell—and the results from this seemingly endless line of credit have not been pretty.

Prices on the necessities are up. But rising prices are nothing new per se—they are the norm. It is not simply that prices are going up today. It is that they are expected to go up. But this expectation of increased prices has little to do with actual supply and demand of goods and services. Via the complex market economy, these goods and services are denominated in the monetary unit of exchange. Increasing this money supply distorts numeric prices, all other factors aside, causing said prices to rise. However, some prices rise before others. And what is truly amazing today is the common misnomer that inflation is a zero-sum game, that there are no winners or losers (which is anything but the case).

This monetary inflation hasn't always been around, and the service-sector economy was by far the dominant force in expansion, for it "acted" just as one would expect under less constrained market conditions—it serviced the producers of the economy and was limited in scope. In fact, just a few decades ago, one parent's income was sufficient to support the family, and working in a factory or a manufacturing plant was more than common. Prices, when they did move, actually went down!

These seemingly wide varieties of economic and political "issues" are actually all linked to one common denominator. The development is all too telling. Prices are up, income is down. And more work has to be done to boot. What is the cause of this phenomenon that has taken shape? Where are the factories? Why are things so expensive? Why do both mom AND dad have to work? Many answers have been given, but more often than not, most of the reasons offered are simply false, or less than comprehensive. Many of these reasons are based on illogical arguments that usually stem from emotionally-charged myths. Some of the prevailing wisdom does draw upon truth, but when it does, typically fails at adequately explaining hugely observable "have our cake and eat it too" events: Rising prices, a shrinking middle class, diminished savings, mammoth trade deficits, artificially-low interest rates, and exuberant government borrowing. These widespread events are very much interrelated, and while not often referenced—all stem from one common root. They represent a pattern of poverty that can be traced back to a single source: The Federal Government's continual debasement of the nation's currency.

Inflation is the cause, and though this word is often times ill defined—it is the common ill which has created the degradation of prosperity in the United States. At its core, inflation is merely the increase in the supply of money, and it is this phenomenon and definition which will be used to explain the real reason behind the economic problems in our national society today. And rightfully so, for it is a monetary problem, as monetary measures connect every transaction made in America. Thus, if the market economy is based on exchange, millions of exchanges every day, then what could be more logical for the outward dilapidation of our economy, if the very money used to make these exchanges is poisoned with continual dilution? The source of these problems is money—printing press money.

Our money's debasement is the underpinning to our country's lack of production, and the jobs and income that privately dissipate with it. Politicians have long offered their various reasons for this decline—this purging of the industrial heartland, but most of these explanations are just as insolvent as the Federal Government and its connected bankers. At the heart of the matter, lies our Federal Government's lust for power. As the surest means to obtain such power lies a method practiced by governments old and new, democratic or totalitarian—the de facto ability to debase the medium of exchange. Beneath this historical push is the law of finding the path of least resistance, for inflation permits a more stealthy growth of non-market authority with far less opposition to the power that assumes it.

Power consumes—for what is power but the ability to alleviate one's own discomfort without choosing the market way, that of effort and labor, by avoiding production, by avoiding work and effort, by living off another's energy. By dictating the use of another's property. There is no greater means of achieving this end than the control of a society's money. However, there are direct consequences. Over time, this inflationary power has had the effect of exponentially liquidating the American manufacturing base. It has caused untold economic depressions, and as an end in itself, it has led to a colossal military presence around the globe. No longer does the United States produce. Through the cloak of inflation, its government and its hired banks have looted the American manufacturer, and while doing so, shifted the entire structure of the domestic economy into the world's first goliath, all-consuming nation. Its economy is a roller-coaster ride of booms and sudden, often times violent depressions, while a mounting bureaucracy increasingly mooches from the labor that is left, justifying at least part of this escalation on foreign "security" abroad. Though this status cannot last, the process has strapped the vast majority of the American public with thin income. Burdened with debt, little wiggle room remains for many Americans to improve their own lives in the immediate days to come. In the future, the situation will become worse. Before the first steps of correcting this course can be taken, many more must realize the source of the misfortune and how it came to be.

The Fundamentals: Markets vs. Government Planning

As was mentioned, around the country a repeat question is asked: *Where are all the jobs?* But when people refer to the word "jobs", they usually aren't referencing employment at the nearest McDonald's. They have something in mind—jobs that pay well, jobs that provide a higher income. Jobs that make life better. While not a prerequisite, these type of jobs—or middle-class jobs—have traditionally been in manufacturing or industry that is capital intense, and yields longer term productive returns. Typically, these forms of employment are rewarding, not only for the individual, but for the family. And so the question lingers, *where are these types of jobs*?

To understand the question, *where have the jobs gone*, or better yet, *where has the production gone*, we must first understand why we work, why we produce, and of course, why we have jobs to begin with. In doing this, the backwards philosophy that has overtaken Washington—that jobs are an end in themselves—becomes ever-more evident. What seems obvious has become more obscured, especially when considering some of the more recent solutions government policy of "stimulus" has offered. Before these pressing concerns can be addressed though, questions that drive to the core of our country's economic sickness, we must first understand a few basics.

Looking back over the past few decades of the American timeline, it is not difficult to realize the dramatic downward shift towards economic poverty. It seems as if resources have become fleeting. Americans often conjecture if Mother Earth has given its last breath to humanity; for the commodities of the world appear to be shrinking in plenty. But this perception though is a perception denominated in dollars. In other words, the development of commodities only appears to diminish through the eyeglass of a falling dollar.

First though, to better lay-out the framework of this book, a distinction must be made between government and private activities. Properly defining these different spheres plays a large role in conceptually delineating what is and what is not a product of the market economy. For today, many misconceptions abound about business efforts vis-a-vis government efforts. It is naïve to equate government work on any level with business efforts. This is a very important distinction to be made; for the nature of "active" government solutions has led much of the public to tolerate further interventions into the market economy.

Business commerce, or work done through voluntary means, gains and employs revenue through the voluntary exchange of goods or services. As such, success can be measured in a very objective way. Efficient productivity is peacefully rewarded by an increase in consumer investment.

Conversely, failure is equally measurable—when a business ceases to serve the consumer, the consumer will cease to patronize the business. To maximize business revenue is to maximize consumer preference. Under this voluntary umbrella of exchange, each participating producer always tends to serve the sovereign individual. So long as property can be used as the individual values, free markets and the infinite choices that go with them materialize in spectacular fashion. It is through this competitive nature of market forces which renders more capital into the hands of those whose talents and efforts best serve the consumer. In this sense, the consumer commands the market economy, and even the largest titans of industry are beholden to their needs and desires.

Government has no such feature. Government is force. It gains revenue through the coercive seizure of private property. Because of this inherent characteristic, the continued encroachment upon private property rights on which government life depends, there remains no objective way to measure success or failure. Any "mission statement" to the contrary will be entirely arbitrary—and because government revenue stems from the involuntary nature of taxes (a word meaning burdensome), there is no immediate "gauge" as to how and when to pursue or cease various government enterprises. It follows that when government increases taxation, it increases the use of coercive force. When government dictates rules and regulations about the disposition of private property, it does so again, by force. And so in terms of addressing our immediate questions on "economy", it is useless to equate government income (or jobs), something inherently derived from force, with those evolving from voluntary exchange—as the underlying concern from our perspective is the market economy. Once this reality is accepted, we can clearly define "jobs" with a prerequisite function of production under voluntary means. By default, this definition eliminates government "make-work" as something that logically, can never solve an epidemic of "no jobs".

After all, people do not work just to work. We do not slave away all day long, away from our families or the comforts of home because we necessarily "want to". One must add value to another in order to receive value in return. Consequently, work is not an end in itself—work is a means to an end. This end is income, or the provisioning of sustenance for life. But the producer has an end—"satisfy the consumer", just as the consumer has an end as well— "reward those producers who best satisfy my needs and wants." Government policy of make-work or this so-called "stimulus" cannot solve a problem that only addresses the means to such an end, for make-work by its very characterization is simply creating more work and labor than what the market economy demands. If the government begins paying people to dig holes, work is done that need not be done. Overall, time and effort are wasted, for the government's policy produced nothing that the consumer valued. On the contrary, not only did the efforts fail to add value, but this government enterprise expropriated the resources involuntarily in order to achieve this failure.

Income, or incoming resources, is what is received when individuals *trade* for their labor. When the consumer trades with the producer, income is provided. Trade then always has two parties of exchange, and this is vital to note—no one loses in trade. In any voluntary transaction, both parties to the trade profit, otherwise the trade does not take place. We are used to the terms producer and consumer, but in a sense, both parties in any trade "double" as producer *and* consumer. The man who owns the convenient store produces his service of distributing milk, but he also consumes part of his profits to employ his labor and time in service to his patrons. The patron which gives his income to consume the milk has first produced income in which to trade. Both parties have at minimum, produced labor at the time of transaction. Enter involuntary methods, and this cannot be said. Government does not produce labor—it takes from labor. Hence, government cannot "trade", for at least one end of government always by necessity acts through force, regardless of whether private individuals involved desire to "trade" or "not to trade". In essence, government can never be a true substitute in either party that accompanies a trade, for government always consumes on both ends of the economic equation. It can never produce. Trade then can only accompany private individuals, be they many or few.

Furthermore, individuals always will tend to prefer more income to less, and less work to more. What individuals earn through jobs represents merely the participation towards a greater division of labor. Under the market economy, an income from a job is received because the work that is done is valued by someone else more than the resources exchanged for it. Income is not an end in itself—it is only a means to the greater end of service to one another. If though, government policy is directed towards only the means, by directly providing said income to the individual, it necessarily tends to decay the ends upon which trade would otherwise bring about. The government consumes resources without first producing, and allocates its consumption towards only further consumption. It subtracts production from the entire "exchange".

Consequently then, for jobs to exist which provide production, they must be based exclusively on this principle of trade, for the other way of planning by force brings about an impossible means by which to calculate success, and a general lowering of productive efforts. This fundamental productive effect, sprung from free trade, deploys greater resources for all involved, and the more developed (and subsequently earned), the more life is generally made more prosperous on the whole. No matter what "social class" the individual may be categorized in the present, over the long term, the standard of existence for the entire population is improved. Individuals can spend more time on leisure, with families—or with other activities that are given greater preference than continued "work". A plethora of choices are created, and more opportunity. All the while, people need to spend less time figuring out how to survive the next day, and can instead, live it. In essence, more time can be spent not laboring, but specializing, choosing, and innovating. All fruits of added forward thinking.

This also brings us about to the foundation of the market economy: Prices. Prices arise after a uniform, highly marketable commodity becomes a standard of measurement by which to compare all other goods by. Through the increase in voluntary trade, a medium of exchange arises in which all other goods bought and sold are "priced" at, giving way to more uniform economic calculation. A yardstick of exchange arises, and money is brought onto the market. Supply and demand of goods and services increase or decrease the price afforded to these goods or services by the accumulative effect of individual valuations. Much has been written about government policy and its effect on the supply and demand of economic goods offered on the market, but few works have examined the effect from government policies on the other side of prices, the monetary side. In other words, prices not only come about from the supply and demand of goods, but also the supply and demand of money, or the media of exchange which the complex market economy brings about to carry on voluntary, elaborate trade.

Of particular note, one of the largest fallacies committed by mainstream intellectuals, regarding monetary prices, has been to "equate" goods with each other. That is, if a gallon of milk costs 3 dollars, then it is presumed that the gallon of milk equals 3 dollars. Not so because they are not equal, as both parties in the exchange profit under any one exchange. The consumer trades his 3 dollars for a gallon of milk, precisely because they are not equal. The consumer values the gallon of milk MORE than his 3 dollars. Conversely, the owner of the convenient store exchanges his gallon of milk for 3 dollars, once again, due to this inequality. The owner of the store selling the milk values the 3 dollars more than his gallon of milk. The exchange takes place, and both parties profit. Conditions of equality would leave no exchange.

But then, why do prices keep rising? Under unhampered market conditions, prices always tend to go down. Market forces place a downward trajectory upon the "cost" of living. As individuals develop resources voluntarily, they are conserved, they are saved. As was pointed out earlier, a natural order of forward thinking continues, and the supply of savings increasingly affords a greater abundance of goods and services. The "price" per unit of resource (or good and service) becomes cheaper. If the apple farmer harvests ten apples per day instead of two, the price per apple will tend to drop—yet the apple farmer's profits, in spite of the lower price per apple, will typically increase with his productive gains (of course, a large factor left out in this simple scenario is the apple farmer's own valuation on his added labor versus his increased return). With the ability to produce more apples, the apple farmer achieves more income, while the consumer achieves a lower price.

This increase in productivity results from the accumulation of capital, one of the defining features of the market economy. Entrepreneurs chase profits, and consumers chase lower prices. But so long as private property rights are not infringed, this process will continue to bring about a higher standard of living for all, even those who are not involved, who are not "chasing" anything. The continual search for profits on the part of these market entrepreneurs forces even those businessmen who are more reluctant in their profit-seeking (and prefer to do less labor) to either leave the market and free-up capital resources for others, or correspondingly increase their own productivity. Conversely, consumers who are not looking for lower prices will find that lower prices result anyway, and their own standard of living increases, even with complete inactivity on their part.

The Analogy

Let me tell you a story, a story of an island with a small population. The island's name is Production Island, and its inhabitants are hard workers, very skilled at making widgets. Over the course of time, the residents of Production Island become so efficient at making these widgets that the demand for their product reaches the world over. The entire world demands widgets from Production Island, for their widget product is the highest quality and the lowest price. Production Island trades its widgets for foreign goods and services, and soon these widgets fetch more and more foreign goods in return. Production Island becomes prosperous. Other nations ship the island food, materials, and supplies in exchange for the island's well-manufactured widgets. Foreign ships constantly fill the island's ports, unloading their imports and replacing their cargoes with the island's widget product.

Foreign demand for widgets increases. To meet this demand, more individuals on Production Island begin to open up businesses making widgets, and as a result, these entrepreneurs hire more of the island's residents. More and more of the island's inhabitants leave their older forms of employment, opting instead to take these better paying jobs making widgets. As more foreigners demand widgets, more resources on the island are shifted into widget making, increasing the supply of the island's widget total. Widget making on Production Island becomes more profitable, and hence, more islanders invest their time and effort into widget making. To make more widgets, more capital must first be placed into increased manufacturing, and to produce at this new level, more of this capital must also be "shared" or offered to fellow islanders, in order for them to leave their older jobs and take the newly offered widget roles. As a result of this increased, yet productive labor, the supply of widgets also increases, and with it, the time to produce each widget falls. More and more are made, and because of this, the price—or cost to produce each widget—begins to fall. As this productive effort continues to unfold, the entire island's standard of living begins to go up. Given more time, capital naturally accumulates, and even those individuals on the island not taking part directly in the widget production indirectly benefit from this increase of capital investment. For example, a butler or a waitress must now be offered higher wages in order to "keep" them from opportunities arising at a widget factory's increase in production. In other words, in order to withdraw their part-take in widget making, higher offers must be made for even the non-widget personnel. All other factors aside, the standard of living gets better. This is Production Island.

Now imagine that some of the islanders decide to store some of their widget production. As the islanders have increasingly mastered the productive process of their widgets, their production time has shortened. The islanders learn to produce more widgets for future shipments, and store these future widgets in warehouses.[1] Foreigners begin to accept simple receipts from these stored and warehoused widgets, for delivery when they are needed in the future. Foreigners continue their shipments of goods and products, but because of various reasons—logistical costs, security issues, or matters of convenience—foreigners accept a simple storage receipt from the islanders for immediate payment. These receipts accepted by the foreigners represent their claim to the produced widgets, safely warehoused away on the island for future use or shipment. Instead of loading foreign cargo ships immediately with the widget product, many widgets are now stacked away inside these new warehouses for safekeeping, until foreigners are ready for their deliveries from the island.

Sooner or later, one of the islanders gets an idea—and begins issuing more receipts for which he has widgets produced and stored in his warehouse. This fraudulent practice catches on, and in deviation from their honest efforts thus far, many of the other islanders follow suit, accepting more foreign goods yet providing these foreigners with receipts above and beyond the amount of widgets saved and stored in their own warehouses. They'll get around to producing more widgets, sooner or later. This behavior not only becomes the norm, it becomes institutionalized.

Moreover, many islanders find it more attractive to quit making widgets altogether—and simply embark on the construction of warehouses with nothing in them. After all,

---

[1] Rothbard, Murray. *What Has Government Done to Our Money?: and, The Case for a 100 Percent Gold Dollar*. Fifth ed. Auburn, Ala.: Ludwig Von Mises Institute, 2005. p.51. Rothbard references the origin of banks on the market as "money warehouses".

foreigners are continuing to accept their warehouse receipts, and the supply of foreign goods seems to be forthcoming. Because of this widespread behavior, many of the island's skilled widget work force, highly-trained from years of production, become increasingly displaced. Building empty warehouses is now demanded, but this elementary, mindless task can easily be performed by even the most rudimentary worker on the island. In the form of income, fewer resources are afforded for this unproductive warehouse building activity.

Consequently, more workers must find a new role, and as the foreigners continue their shipments in exchange for ever-fraudulent receipts, the distribution and shuffling of the massive glut of foreign goods and products has now over taken the island. In exchange for the "printed" warehouse receipts, which now abound among the island's consuming population, these displaced workers fill these new service positions. Warehouse receipts are paid out to these former widget workers, who now man the countless distribution and retail stores in the shape of department clerks and underutilized security guards. Yet it requires more and more warehouse receipts to purchase all of these goods for themselves, for before these dislodged, yet once proud, widget workers receive their own receipts, the warehouse owners of course, have already issued a new wave of receipts. For they alone have the privilege of the printing press.

And all the while, the day lurks when the foreigners will wake to the grim reality, there are no widgets in the warehouses. This has been the transformation of the American economy, one of production and savings, to one of spend-thrift and consumption. One of Production Island to Consumer Continent.

Basic Origins of Money

To understand how this inflation of "receipts" comes about, and the production of widgets gives way to warehouses, we must understand the nature of money itself. Furthermore, we must understand sound money, versus government-enforced fiat currency.

Money comes about its formation only through voluntary market exchange. Moreover, money can only originate as a commodity, or something that has intrinsic value, commonly demanded by producers and consumers alike. Hence, money can never originate from government decree, or *fiat*.

Ludwig von Mises, an early 20th century economist, pioneered what has now come to be recognized as the Austrian School of Economics. Mises deduced this logical concept of money formation in his early economic work—now known as *Regression Theorem*.[2] Building on Carl Menger's 19th century work, Mises realized that money must first come about as a commodity, and paper through market exchange only later evolves as a certificate, or a "receipt", backed by a commodity, or which is redeemable in said commodity. Paper on the market is only a claim of real property, but money can never originate as paper. Therefore, it can only become pure paper—

---

[2] Mises, Ludwig Von. *The Theory of Money and Credit*. New Haven: Yale UP, 1953.

that is, redeemable for nothing—*after* the complex market economy has grown used to trading paper certificates backed by a commodity, namely precious metals. History has typically shown that over time, governments, inherently inclined towards the demolition of private property, tend to monopolize the mint, separating the paper certificate from its commodity claim. Typically, this happens simply by declaring it to be, by fiat decree.

However in early stages, as the market economy becomes increasingly complex, moving from localized barter-trade to wider money-transactions, there is an integrated tendency for markets to move towards a more uniform media of exchange. In essence, money is demanded on the market only because of this increased complexity of voluntary trade. Under situations of extreme poverty, where resources are extraordinarily scarce, survival is the number one goal of the individual. The priority is first and foremost, finding the resources to sustain life. Poverty then is defined by a lack of resources. Under impoverished conditions, little or no trade can exist, because the few resources available are entirely consumed by the individual or family. The individual must consume entirely what little he can produce just to stay alive. It is only after the individual masters the laborious day, that he or she can save, or abstain from immediate consumption, thereby giving rise to the potential of trade.[3] When the individual can finally set aside part of his daily

[3] Mises, Ludwig Von. Human Action: A Treatise on Economics. Auburn, Ala: Ludwig Von Mises Institute, 2008. p. 529. Mises quips that those who would abolish interest rates "would very soon throw mankind back into the original state of natural poverty." A

intake for perhaps a better meal or a better roof down the road, resources become more developed, and *savings* come into existence. The rise of savings then sets the stage for fist barter, and then finally, a demand for "common barter", or the use of a common media of exchange (i.e. money).

As discussed, by its classical definition, inflation is merely the increase in the supply of money. Governments from time immemorial have justified their control of the medium of exchange and then naturally, debased the currency as a concealed technique of increasing their regime's revenue. The United States is no exception to this trend. Throughout the 20th Century, the Federal Government paid for wars, government programs, and a host of other large expenses, not through direct taxation, but by merely printing more US dollars. Legal tender laws eventually were ingrained into the American economy—laws that decreed certain forms of payment had to be accepted—and through this process of monopolizing the mint, hard money became forced out by government paper.

This conception, known as *Gresham's Law*, has been cited by many of the leading proponents of the Austrian School of Economics, such as Ludwig von Mises and later Murray Rothbard, who correctly concluded that bad money forces good money out of circulation because of government's overvaluation of the "bad money". When government insists that one paper dollar, redeemable for nothing, must be

---

recurrent theme in Mises' work was an emphasis on the natural scarcity of goods, and that mankind originates in a state of poverty.

accepted for payment at the same rate as one silver dollar, sooner or later, silver dollars will cease to circulate. If one can pay for a cheeseburger at McDonald's with a one dollar paper bill, versus a one ounce silver coin (which the government says is equal in value to the paper bill), most people are likely to conclude they'd rather part with the paper, and keep the silver. For an excellent analysis on Gresham's Law, see Murray Rothbard's short work, *What has Government Done to our Money?*[4]

It often takes time for individuals to initially accept government intervention. For instance, as a means to help pay for the American Civil War, legal tender laws were introduced in order to force private individuals to accept Lincoln's "greenbacks" as payment—or printed paper notes, which could not be immediately redeemed for gold or silver. During the War Between the States, these government IOU's were issued en-masse, and quickly depreciated in value. It took more than a decade for the Federal Government to repeal these new monetary laws, and in order to honor the glut of Lincoln paper, the money supply had to undergo a large contraction during Reconstruction. Though the greenback was finally done away with, the agitation for fiat money continued.

By 1933, not only were legal tender laws put firmly back into place, but all domestic dollar notes were "freed" from their ties to gold. Not only was the classical gold standard done away with, but gold was nationalized by the American government, its private ownership outlawed in exchange or contract, the

---

[4] Rothbard, p. 72-75

bulk of the country's gold stock seized and deposited with the Federal Reserve Banking System. And shortly thereafter, with Europe in shambles after the Second World War and many nations in debt, the US emerged as the western successor to the British Empire. This new found political and military clout provided incredible monetary advantages, as the world's financial center was transferred from London to New York. The US dollar became the new reserve currency, and though domestic exchange was now prohibited with gold (after Franklin Roosevelt said so), foreign nations and central banks were still capable of exchanging their dollar reserves for gold bullion, at the fixed rate of $35 / ounce.

Fast forward some two decades later and American economic hegemony had already attempted to take advantage of its monetary influence, inflating the dollar to pay for both the Vietnam War and the new mega programs of the Great Society (Medicare and Medicaid). Once this inflation became apparent to foreigners, more and more overseas creditors exchanged the now overvalued dollars for gold. Gold reserves in the United States shrank, and as more foreigners called in their American notes, more gold reserves left the country. And as we already know the end of this dollar run, this outpouring of precious metals culminated with the final American response to "close the gold window". Rather than shrink the money supply, the US response was financial default; by 1971—the last remaining thread to American sound money was no more.

Today, nothing stands in the way of further inflation. Since this beginning of the fiat era, or the age of pure paper money, inflation has wrecked its havoc throughout the US economy, frustrating market exchange and bringing about countless boom and bust periods (the rampant inflation of the 1970s brought with it a decade of recession). With the collapse of the last gold tie, another occurrence came about, one that has been applauded by politicians and misguided scholars alike. The reserve currency of the world—at one time promised to be "as good as gold"—was now positioned as the "I promise" US dollar. That is to say, for the first time in history, a world network of banks and sovereign nations rested entirely on a paper money system, all foreign currencies and central banks entrenched to the American money of fiat. At the mercy of centralized government, the "good-as-gold" dollar is a distant memory.

Prosperity under the Gold Standard

As an easily portable precious metal, gold naturally arose within markets as the uniform media of exchange. Gold is a scarce commodity, easily portable, malleable, and in complex economies of numerous transactions, it has evolved to command value on the market—serving as a solid "storage" of wealth. Over great lengths of time, the supply and demand of gold is also naturally steady. In relation to other commodity goods, changes in either are easily communicated via the market economy. You can't print more gold.

That being said, fiat paper money never arises on the market to serve as a media of exchange, but only until later, when the government separates certificate from commodity. This is the history of money and it is a history ripe of governments high-jacking the confidence of the market and replacing the root of market confidence with paper. The commodity is typically debased or divorced entirely, and the remaining paper certificates, though able to linger on in exchange, become ever devalued. But with all paper money, without its original foundation, eventually this confidence collapses.

As we have already discussed, our own Federal Government slowly but deliberately separated the gold-backed notes from the gold itself. This was not done through the voluntary market, but through force. This principle is critical to understand if we are to also understand the concept of monetary imperialism. Prior to the dawn of the 20th century, nearly all sovereign nations were on some sort of gold or silver standard. Gold was the international and uniform media of exchange. All domestic currencies merely represented different weights in gold. For example, the dollar was nothing more than 1/20th of a gold ounce; the British pound sterling, the French franc, the German mark— were all redeemable at their respective domestic banks for gold coin (In the United States, one could literally walk into a bank and swap 20 dollars for a gold ounce).

For clear reasons, governments and their central banks have always tried to inflate the money supply as much as they could get away with. This "hard' discipline prevented independent governments from inflating their currencies; if the government or its central bank did, individuals and depositors simply exchanged the inflated notes for gold, forcing their respective governments (or privileged bankers) to halt the printing presses.

By the latter part of the 19th Century, the world economy flourished under the classical gold standard, which through a genuine division of labor, ever-widened the benefits of the industrial revolution. Though each country still issued its own national currency, the backing of gold created a uniform standard, or a uniform media-of-exchange. After all, this is one of the sole purposes of money on the market to begin with! A standard commodity which is widely accepted by all to facilitate voluntary exchange! Competition was strengthened and Adam Smith's division of labor provided the development of international resources, bringing access to more capital and goods to more people, and breaking through the barrier of arbitrary national borders to do so.[5]

But the classical gold standard had one more benefit. The same hard discipline which checks government's tendency to inflate also does the same via international trade. For instance, all other factors aside, if the French inflated the number of their francs in circulation, French prices would increase. With the rise in prices, French goods become more "expensive" when denominated in Francs; French exports to other nations suffer and more imported goods would flood into France (foreign goods remember are untouched in numeric price due to their denomination in their respective national currencies). Voila! French consumers now assess foreign goods as "cheaper" compared to their domestic French counterparts. Foreign countries—say Britain— would experience an export boom in the French market—but this practice was typically short lived. Eventually, foreign countries would demand payment in gold, as they themselves have no use for French francs. This becomes especially so after the French inflation becomes readily

---

[5] Smith, Adam. *The Wealth of Nations*. Ed. Edwin Cannan. New York: Modern Library, 1994. p. 458. Smith describes the wealth of a society to rest on more unrestricted international exchange, and debunks the mercantilist notion of the time that a nation must interfere with foreign trade in order to prevent gold and silver from leaving the country to satisfy the balance of payments that may arise from importing more goods than what are exported.

apparent (and foreigners realize there are more French franks floating around).[6]

Under the classical gold standard, any country which pursued this practice of national counterfeiting would stand to lose a fortune in real wealth rather quickly. Furthermore, since all currencies were merely representations of various amounts of gold, the residents of each country could specialize in their individual production preferences—in what they did best (as determined by the international consumer). In the absence of currency debasement, transparent voluntary exchange "pushed" labor and entrepreneurial effort, and due to geographical or demographic considerations, different economic activities developed whereby these diverse populations maintained a *comparative advantage*. Utilizing their respective resources at hand to specialize in goods and services demanded abroad by foreigners, trade could achieve the goods they did not possess, but wanted or needed in return. There could be no shortcuts to prosperity though. Frenchmen had to offer the Swiss something of value to the Swiss, or the British had to produce goods the Spanish consumer voluntarily desired, i.e. no "rip-offs". All of this international exchange took place at face value, absent the nationalized fraud of currency manipulation, counterfeiting, or fiat paper deception.

To underscore the point more clearly, think of the commercial progress of the United States. One overlooked but noteworthy reason Americans prospered internally was that

6 Rothbard, *What has Government done to our Money?* p.99. Referencing David Hume's 18th century work, Rothbard makes an analogy under the classical gold standard—and demonstrates how the international balance of payments checks sovereign inflation.

commerce has been facilitated with uniform, but *hard money*, media-of-exchange. Throughout all states of the union, one currency had been utilized, creating a smooth system of trade. It would likely be unimaginable if one US state imposed taxes against the imported goods of another; so too would it be illogical if the several states of the union issued their own independent currencies. In this manner, it can be seen that government-issued fiat money can restrict trade internationally in the same manner as a tariff, or other artificially-induced government barrier to exchange. Imagine if each of the 50 states issued its own fiat currency, having them "float" against one another. American internal commerce would be chaotic and thrust into confusion. The uniformity of the dollar made it possible for one business in Virginia to exchange goods with another business in California, without the insane calculations of currency swaps. But this uniformity is brought about by the market, not by government. Market money innately tends towards a uniform, commonly accepted commodity, one that always tends to serve more readily in this capacity of complex exchange (as already mentioned, this is at the heart of Mises' Regression Theorem).

In fact, the country's founding document, the US Constitution, only grants authority to the Federal Government to coin money, and explicitly forbids any state from introducing its own currency. It goes further and clearly restricts government from introducing or enforcing legal tender laws, while specifically naming the market's choice of hard money. Many of the Founders were deeply troubled with the prospect of fiat money, which had proven to be a disaster during the Revolution. As a result, gold and silver were explicitly commanded. The first paragraph of Article I, Section 10 reads:

No State shall enter into any Treaty, Alliance, or Confederation; grant Letters of Marque and Reprisal; coin Money; emit Bills of Credit; make any Thing but gold and silver Coin a Tender in Payment of Debts; pass any Bill of Attainder, ex post facto Law, or Law impairing the Obligation of Contracts, or grant any Title of Nobility.

No doubt this clause stems from the earlier American experience with the Continental dollar, issued during the Revolution to finance war efforts—but quickly becoming worthless not long after introduction.

Under this light, one can imagine the economic chaos ensuing from various state governments engaged in their own currency wars, replacing market money by issuing fiat paper, inflating ad hoc. Commerce would be artificially disrupted and the standard of living would inevitably plummet. This scenario was prevented from being orchestrated on an "en-masse" level by the uniform gold standard, which overcame any such trade barrier and which deepened the division of labor between separated geographic distances. Underneath the umbrella of gold-based exchange, this system of uniformity provided a smooth and natural way for transactions to take place on international markets. This system of ease, using the market's choice of money, spread the benefits of the division of labor across national borders—increasing prosperity for an ever growing number of people. Less work had to be done to achieve greater living standards, perhaps benefiting the poor the most, shoving incomes up and expanding the middle class in a more timely way (this would become especially true at the onset of the Industrial Revolution). The market's choice of money uniformly interconnected sovereign economies, and the fruits of production were more widely received.

Part II

Economic Depression

Fiat Money and the Business Cycle

Perhaps the most significant, yet grossly misunderstood economic trend is the so called "Business Cycle". The confusion and mass depression of the cycle causes not just economic poverty, but extreme social strife. Because of the misunderstanding about its source, central government has often used this friction to consolidate its position as "more important" in solving the very crisis that we will see, government causes to begin with. The disintegration of the gold standard, and the unprecedented growth of concentrated power in Washington, is fixed in a failure to comprehend the causes of economic depressions. This swelling of government intervention, especially into monetary matters, has largely been achieved precisely because of the social turmoil brought on by the business cycle, and the boom-bust result that it brings. Thus, correctly assessing the business cycle is also critical to identify how the United States has gone from making widgets to solely consuming them—and why this fundamentally flawed system of paper will inevitably fail.

The continual ups and downs within our modern rollercoaster economy are often pointed to by many today as a failure of unfettered "greedy" capitalism—not a new conclusion for sure, as the infamous reason given by John Maynard Keynes was "animal spirits", a less than sufficient answer, but one that indicates that the boom and later recession happen out of irrational frenzy (more on Keynes later). But in understanding the causes of this cycle, and the inevitable economic depressions that come with them, the wild boom surely is not grounded in capitalism. And the source certainly does not originate with arbitrary greed, for depressions do not sporadically occur because of some illusory yet coincidental effort by masses of people who suddenly cease "buying"—or as the common quip alludes to—"Well, people just aren't spending money out there." The true cause of our economic roller coaster ride stems from an opaque institution known as the Federal Reserve. This quasi-government creature not only orchestrates the "booms" and "busts" we are familiar with, but it also makes possible the national government's colossal debt. While our country's central bank may not seem very significant to your daily life, it's crucial Americans begin to pay more attention.

All of our past economic depressions or "busts" in our lifetime were caused because the Federal Reserve increased the nation's supply of money. Though hidden through complex bureaucratic terminology, the conceptual process is quite straightforward. To "stimulate" the economy, or seemingly grant a false euphoria, the Federal Reserve utilizes its money printing tools to artificially lower interest rates. IOU checks are written by the Fed to the nation's largest and most politically-connected banks, and with a few keystrokes of the computer, money is created out of thin air. These big banks gain more cash on hand, profiting by having the privilege of being the first recipient of "new money". Remember though, all this newly granted cash is counterfeit. These reserves represent zero new resources produced and saved from economic growth. However, with the creation of new money, central bankers give the appearance that more savings are available for investment—that people have abstained from consumption in the present, relinquishing increased resources for other uses. And so begins the boom. It should be noted, this counterfeiting bank cartel is purely a product of government. There is nothing "free market" about it.

When something is more plentiful or abundant, the price tends to fall. This is also true of the interest rate, which plummets as the supply of paper money increases. After the Fed injects counterfeit reserves into the vaults of its member banks, the price of this diluted capital now appears cheaper. But critical to what has actually taken place, all of the genuine resources in the economy have been watered-down by the government counterfeit. The interest rate does not fall because of an increase in voluntary savings; but through government intervention. The Federal Reserve simply fixes the price.

The new counterfeit money now makes its way into the economy from the banking system, typically first appearing through the loan markets. In the process, the Fed deceives businessmen and entrepreneurs, who because of the lower interest rates, are falsely signaled more resources are available to invest in longer term projects. These artificially cheap interest rates cause banks to make more business loans, and more credit is granted. As a result, more projects are started, and more investments are made. Politicians in office are praised for healthy economic prosperity. But it's simply an illusion, all of it pure fantasy.

It is important to note here that the boom phase is the unhealthy stage where the economy grows sick. All of these new investment projects cannot be sustained, as consumers never actually demanded any of them. Once the money-printing scheme ceases, the bust phase sets in. All of these businesses or projects are now realized to be, in fact *malinvestments* and they must be liquidated (i.e. an overabundance of houses which no one demanded be built). Businesses close. Mass unemployment is created—all at once. These recessions are painful but necessary for true healthy economic growth to resume in the country. Trying to sustain the boom is equal to trying to keep the economy sick. The government's "counterfeit" merely diluted scarce resources, eventually causing real capital to become misallocated, squandered, and ultimately wasted. The situation just outlined has been the plague of our American economy.

Over time, this has caused mammoth distortions throughout the US economy and has borne enormous malinvestments with existing pre-boom capital. And if government becomes even more interventionist after the bust, economic depressions can hang around for years—as markets are prevented from clearing and liquidating these malinvestments. Since the birth of the central counterfeiting machine, it is relatively straightforward to see the domestic squandering of real capital caused by the Fed-driven "boom and bust" cycle. Because of this Fed counterfeiting, the American economy has been repeatedly subjected to a series of malinvestments which have severely restrained true economic growth. Since every transaction in the economy is done through the common medium of exchange, the manipulation of markets is best achieved through the tampering with the money supply. Interest rates—or the rate at which time is coordinated with investment—can be superficially altered if the central banking manipulator can give borrowers the short-run prospect that the pool of resources has grown. Nominal interest rates fall, and all other factors aside, consumption increases in the present. Since a boost in consumption is immediately felt and seen by more of the public, a euphoric feeling of "wealth" gives the impression of true prosperity.

It is of course fiction, but this fictional appearance can indeed be provided via the injection of large amounts of new dollar reserves through the cartelized banking system. In order to understand the other detrimental effects on productive activities in the market economy, let us examine in more detail this domestic boom-bust process.

Domestic Boom and Bust: The Plague of the US Economy

As mentioned, the boom-bust process has been detailed by several astute, but largely ignored economists throughout the 20th Century. Perhaps the most notable, and until late the most neglected of these men have been Ludwig von Mises, Murray Rothbard, and F.A. Hayek. Thanks in no small part to Congressman Ron Paul's heroic efforts of mass education, these true intellectuals are receiving an ever widening audience.

Within many of their works lie the origins of why and how the central bank expands the money supply, typically over and above the aggregate level of voluntary savings.[7] For several reasons given (many of which are obvious), these central planners "print" more and more fiat money. Perhaps it is the fallacious attempt to advance investment, or provide acclaim to

---

7 Rothbard, Murray. *America's Great Depression.* Princeton, NJ: Van Nostrand, 1963. p.169-171. Running up to the 1929 stock market crash, Rothbard explains that the "Roaring 20s" was fostered by the expansion of bank credit, aided by the newly formed Federal Reserve. However, the upward pressure on prices from this increase of the money supply was obscured by real gains in market productivity during this time frame, and the counteracting downward pressure on prices from this expansion of goods and services. Because of simultaneous market forces, such as changing time-preferences, alterations in supply and demand, or shifts in real voluntary savings, inflationary pressure can be difficult to see with the naked eye. Its effects must be logically deduced.

political officials through the phony riches of the boom; perhaps it is to pay for wars, or the welfare state; or the all-too-common motive—to award crony profits to connected special-interest groups, inside or outside banking circles. The political incentives always will ensure a natural tendency to keep interest rates lower than the market rate, and whatever incentive proves victorious—any entity vested with the power to monopolize the supply of money will always tend to use said power. Put in another way, the power of the printing press will always be placed into motion. If we accept the proposition that printing money out of thin air is fraudulent counterfeiting, and leads to theft—regardless of whether it is done by private individuals or the government—it is incumbent upon one to analyze conditions before this widespread notion of central banking was acknowledged as good public policy.[8] For that reason, the environment which existed prior to the centralization of power over the money supply must be scrutinized. Looking at historical life before the era of the American central bank is crucial in this examination, as the current Federal Reserve System has only been around since 1913. Prior to the 20th Century, a period marked by the absence of government FDIC insurance or the lender of last resort, banks largely stood on their own. Subjected to market forces, the phrase "bank run"

---

[8] Deflation, or a contraction of the money supply, can take place as well. But deflation, and rising interest rates, above the market rate, can only take place after a period of inflation. Even with this, deflation typically occurs not as purposeful government policy, but in spite of government policy, as a consequence of the prior boom. As malinvestment from the boom is liquidated, vast quantities of capital investment can disappear, leading to a fall in the stock of money as well. In the long run though, the tendency with fiat money has been continued suppression of interest rate prices.

was enough to shake even the most prevalent captains within the country's banking establishment. During this era, the government-sanctioned system of fractional-reserve banking was prone to these common "panics". If the public caught wind that the local bank had been foolish with their deposits entrusted to it, more and more individuals would rush to the particular over-inflated bank to claim their deposits. In such cases, when the bank was indeed utterly insolvent, it would be unable to meet their contractual demands. Because of this natural, en-masse reaction by the public to the inflated (and insolvent) nature of the fractional-reserve banking system, the expansion of bank credit through this fractional-banking method was "checked" and prevented nationalized insolvency from materializing into the one we see today—one which demands continual public bail-outs.

Essentially, fractional-reserve banking is a practice by which a bank creates new money from thin air. This banking practice has been around in the United States since before the country was officially born, but began to become much more significant in economic terms around the time of the industrial revolution, when more and more people began using banking services to safe-keep their newfound higher incomes. Banks came about on the market out of this convenience and security. However, banks began to learn that government would aid a process whereby some of the deposits from the vault were loaned out to others, without permission from the depositor, while at the same time, providing this money to said depositor for continual use (in the form of a checking account). So if Bob goes and deposits his income at the bank (say gold coins), he receives back paper receipts from the bank (gold coins are onerous to haul around all day, and stuffing them under your pillow is not very secure). The bank then turns around, using Bob's money in their vaults, and loans more receipts to Fred. We can see here that if both Bob and Fred go to the bank to demand gold coins, which supposedly their receipts both represent titles too, the bank will be unable to pay up. But of course, the bank does not expect anyone to notice right away. So all the while, Bob continually uses his bank receipts (or certificates representing his gold coinage in the bank, which is now actually in Fred's hands), to purchase goods and services. Bob is using "fractional" money to purchase goods and services, so this one deposit from Bob multiplies the amount of money in circulation, as Fred too is purchasing goods and services with his receipts. New money has been created from nothing. Eventually, enough bank patrons, seeing local prices begin to rise, and catching wind of the bank's practices, rush to the bank to attempt to collect on their debt owed. Absent government intervention, the bank must pay or liquidate its assets and go out of business (as any other business would).

In addition, inter-bank competition limited this process as well, as anyone who is paid with these receipts from Bank A—who uses a different bank—would deposit these competing receipts for gold claims in their own bank, Bank B. Since Bank B has little use for Bank A's gold receipts, it will eventually call on their competitor to transfer said gold, or "hard money", into its own vaults. This limitation brought on a tendency for banks to compete on standards of reliability, not the other way around. To understand fractional-reserve banking in more detail, see the brilliant work done by Jesus Huerta de Soto, *Money, Bank Credit, and Economic Cycles.*[9]

The patrons of the bank run checked this inflationary embezzlement practice. Of course, markets would force banks to honor their contracts, or close down and liquidate through bankruptcy—like any other insolvent business. Without mass intervention by government, this practice of fractional-reserve embezzlement could never have continued. But the reverse held true, and though it was the banker's fraudulent behavior which caused the phenomena to begin with, government political forces tended to side with the banker's cries of the "panic" that came with the bank run (Of course, bankers have access to lots of cash, which politicians usually find attractive).

By the end of the 19th Century, the banking industry was agitating for "reforms", and this lobbying achieved perhaps the crown jewel of all political perks to date—the Federal Reserve Act. Inherent in this agitation was the listening ear of many government officials. Sympathetic to the banking industry's desire to inflate lays a common interest from government's tendency to do the same. Government officials utilize the

---

[9] De Soto, Jesus Huerta. *Money, Bank Credit, and Economic Cycles.* Trans. Melinda A. Stroup. Second ed. Auburn, Alabama: Ludwig Von Mises Institute, 2009. p.124. De Soto reveals in early historical markets that the misappropriation of bank deposits (without the depositors' consent) was treated as an act of embezzlement or breach of contract. Over time, common contract law governing bank deposits was distorted, due in part to pressure from banking interest groups and sympathetic government officials. This shift in legal status assisted with the proliferation of fractional-reserve banking. Also see Rothbard, *What Has Government Done to Our Money?*, p.52.

depositors' money at banks to finance their own political interests, either domestically or internationally. Bankers have traditionally viewed these government loans as an easy way, in fact a "risk-free" way, to earn income faster and with more ease than what could be earned under natural market conditions. Government has the privilege of confiscating revenue, and does not have the same limitations as commercial investments. The symbiotic relationship between Big Government and Big Banker transcends the ages. And just as many large established businesses have looked to government partnership as a means to gain an advantage over their market competition, by passing regulations to force costs on others, so too did the nation's top bankers look to government to avoid the market's punishment of bank runs on their insolvent fractional-reserve methods.

The Federal Reserve was said to be the "banker's bank", or of course, the lender of last resort. But the debate over a central bank is almost as old as the American Republic itself. This unholy alliance of government and unsound banking was the culmination of Alexander Hamilton's dream, one that Thomas Jefferson had long spurned. This first American debate over monetary policy was a fierce one, for central banking was not just any other piece of legislation. The reality of central banking facilitates the coming together of wide scale corruption, antithetical to a free republic, but perhaps the most overlooked yet simplistic interest and symptom of them all is the perpetual pursuit of a free lunch. But yet, it is highly unlikely that the ramifications from central banking—such as welfarism, the deprivation of capital intense production, increased speculation and stock gambling, or continued war abroad—could first come about without the mass hysteria caused by the business cycle. Only then can government, under the guise of solving the nightmarish mess, achieve a substantial growth in power, set by precedent, which lasts long after the economic depression passes.

As was previously outlined, but necessary to emphasize: The initiation of the business cycle originates when the central bank injects new reserves into its member banks, increasing the supply of "printed" capital throughout the banking system. This initiation can take place explicitly, through the central bank's inflationary mechanisms, such as open market operations. Or implicitly, by the central bank's very existence—which creates a moral hazard of risky behavior that would not otherwise occur (since the opportunity for future bail-outs may exist, etc.).[10] The methods of this credit expansion are numerous, but conceptually the end result is the same—the false impression of more readily usable resources. Since capital now appears more abundant, the price of this watered down resource is cheapened. Interest rates tend to fall—albeit artificially—signaling entrepreneurs that more resources are available for long term investment. More projects begin in the present than what otherwise would. Originating with the banks, the new credit enters the domestic economy through the loan market, and as it does, the prices of capital goods are bid-up.

---

[10] Bagus, Philipp. *The Tragedy of the Euro*. Auburn, Ala.: Ludwig Von Mises, 2010. p.69-76. Bagus summarizes the open market operations of the Fed and the European Central Bank (ECB), and their respective methods of money creation. See also p. 16, where Bagus briefly reviews the moral hazard created by central banking.

Resources—including labor—are stripped away from their former roles, and misallocated to new, unsustainable places—where the consumer never demanded them to be.

Because the additional resources to produce these new investments do not exist, they are unsustainable in the long run. Entrepreneurs have been "fooled"—but do not realize their error until the rate of credit expansion dwindles, and rising interest rates reveal their mistakes. Once this inevitably comes about, the "bust" period of the business cycle replaces the boom, and these unsustainable ventures must be liquidated, while remaining resources are reallocated to places more urgently demanded by consumers. But only after the bust begins are these new investments finally realized to be in fact, malinvestments. It is crucial to remember though that once the boom is initiated from this artificial credit, the bust is inevitable—and the longer the boom is kept afloat, the more severe the corrective bust. The boom therefore is the stage that begins the unhealthy misallocation of capital and the squandering of real savings.

To simplify the concept, we need only to think of a given money supply in the market economy. At any one time, a complex market of voluntary exchange has a given quantity of money within it in order to facilitate the exchange of goods and services. But the total supply of money is really irrelevant in the long run; for money is the only good in the market that produces no social benefit when its quantity is arbitrarily increased (more apples produced generally will produce a cheaper price per apple).[11]

But when the supply of money increases, all other prices generally rise relative to their corresponding "yardstick" of measurement—the supply of money in the market economy. It makes no difference if there are 100 dollars in the market versus 200 dollars; numeric prices will merely reflect that which they are traded through. What causes the chaos is the *transition* between the smaller supply of money and the larger supply of money. This is the real concept of inflation—not the rise in prices, which is a mere symptom of inflation, but the increase in the total supply of the media of exchange.

Under a free market, inflation can rarely occur with "shock and awe". Precious metals typically arrive to serve as the common and uniform media of exchange. Any influx of these metals usually takes place gradually (gold cannot be "printed"; it must be mined and produced through exploration and hard work). Furthermore, because free markets are defined by voluntary exchange, money cannot easily be counterfeited en mass, or dumped into circulation for any sustained period of time without a lofty level of communication to the consumer. In the long run, any bank or "money warehouse" which prints more banknotes over and above its reserve of savings would cease to exist, precisely because of these unreliable, fraudulent practices. An external factor, by inherent design, is necessary to keep this behavior intact.

---

11 Rothbard, *What Has Government Done to Our Money?*, p.39.

If we take the aforesaid example, that a market's given money supply totals 100 dollars to begin with—all prices, including interest rates, will be denominated in dollars based off a total supply of 100 (roughly). But suppose the central bank forces the transition to an increased level of total money, and injects another 50 dollars into the market economy? In the short term, interest rates will appear lower than what they otherwise would, because now the allusion that this "new" fiat money is equivalent to real capital sends signals to market entrepreneurs that more resources are available. The point of origin that the new money enters the economy is via the banks, and all goods and services positioned to receive the new money first from the banks tend to rise in price. This usually is seen to take place in the capital goods market—such as durable consumer goods (houses), raw materials, bulk commodities, or those goods generally used, not for immediate consumption, but to produce goods for later consumption. This price of timing is the critical function the natural rate of interest serves in the market economy. In other words, the rate of interest is the "built-in" measurement used by individuals to coordinate the ratio of resources dedicated towards production versus consumption.

As discussed, once the increased money supply filters throughout the economy and stabilizes to a constant or near constant, prices return to their "pre-boom" levels. Interest rates rise revealing the mistaken allocations of capital made during the boom. Pretend for a moment that the market rate of interest is 6%, but after the Federal Reserve injects counterfeit capital throughout the banking system, this rate of interest "falls" to 3%. Now, imagine that at 6% interest (the market rate), 20 different businesses accept loans to expand their own production. After the Fed's doping measure signals the drop to 3%, say 50 different businesses now decide to finance investments for amplified production.

But all of these different investment projects are still drawing from the same pool of resources. The real total amount of capital never increased, only the amount of counterfeit. At some point, once the flow of this new money eases its way throughout the market, most, if not all, of these projects will go "bust" (even those that did not originally partake will be affected, as their energies were drawn into the misaligned productive structure). This is also why a systematic breakdown of mass bankruptcy occurs—and also why so many people become unemployed, all at the same time. In the end, the malinvestments are not sustainable. Consumers never actually demanded the increased production, as only the government price-fixing caused their initiation.[12]

It should be realized that this experience of repeat economic depression is purely caused through the increase in the supply of money, and that the symptomatic effect when they should not invest—and resources are misallocated away from

---

[12] Rothbard, Murray. *Man, Economy, and State with Power and Market*. Second ed. Auburn, Alabama: Ludwig Von Mises Institute, 2009. p.1000. Also, see Rothbard, *America's Great Depression*, p.8-9. Murray Rothbard emphasized that any explanation of the business cycle must address what he coined as the "cluster of errors" problem; whereby, market entrepreneurs en-masse, skilled for their ability to forecast consumer preferences, simultaneously suffer losses.

consumer wants and demands. Because of this organized sickness known as the boom, stemming from the central planning authorities at the central bank, whole generations of savings of this increase in exchange medium is to discombobulate market timing and coordination. Entrepreneurs invest and hard work are squandered away through unsustainable nation-wide malinvestments.

The Keynesian Curse: The Neglect of Savings and Production

Today, these economic causes of the business cycle are widely ignored. This ignorance is reflected under our Federal Government's pattern of both monetary and direct fiscal policy. This doctrine our central government has perpetuated is regrettable. It is dreadfully unfortunate that supposed educated individuals would adopt economic policy conflicting with one of the greatest products of Western civilization—logic.

Government fiscal stimulus and monetary stimulus are very similar in nature. However, fiscal can be seen more readily, monetary less so. Both policies though focus in on increasing some arbitrary level of consumption, that "aggregate demand" must be boosted, and government is the means to do it (In fact, all that really occurs is that government consumes more in the present, at the expense of future consumption by the public). Monetary intervention though, is perhaps the most harmful. Monetary stimulus, or continual monetization of Federal Government debt, along with artificially low interest rates through the commercial banking sector, are all of course the Federal response to "create employment" and invigorate our country's economic activity through massive government programs aimed at ever-more consumption. But if we remember our analogy, an island that consumes without producing is already lacking the fundamental building-block upon which the market economy rests. Without savings, the pursuit of such stimulative policies will not only fail to achieve said objectives, but like a bad Ponzi scheme—such actions will also serve to damage the nation's economic growth in the long run. These policies only serve to saddle the public with more debt and future sacrifice that need not come about.

This practice by our government does not reflect a new line of thinking though. In all actuality, our economic "booms and busts" over the last several decades certainly echo this. The philosophy of government monetary stimulus, as well as fiscal stimulus, is rooted from misguided early 20th Century economists, chiefly John Maynard Keynes. Many historians refer to Keynes as the "father of modern economics". Put more accurately, he is plainly the father of "bad economics".

Keynes and his followers were not satisfied with the classical school of thought, and this huge deviation was outlined in his master work, *The General Theory of Employment, Interest and Money*—first published in 1936.[13] To a greater degree, Keynes held in contempt Adam Smith's "invisible hand"—that markets, always following self-interest, would create the greatest social benefit. Keynes believed that significant progress could be made if the hand was not so much "invisible", but

---

[13] Keynes, John Maynard. *The General Theory of Employment, Interest and Money.* New York: Harcourt, 1964.

rather "strongly visible". His misunderstanding of the business cycle was perhaps the greatest reason for this failure in logic. Misdiagnosing the sickness, that economic depressions came about because of the increase in the supply of money, Keynes instead subscribed to a theory that governments could lift their nation's economies from recession and "cure" unemployment by deficit spending, and "monetary easing" (government spending of resources it does not have). This deficit spending within private markets would thereby stimulate consumption, which according to the British Lord Keynes, would drive further and further economic growth. In economic jargon, this was his theory of the "multiplier effect". Therefore, government initiates further consumption and the economy is "stimulated" by boosting aggregate demand in a desperate attempt to return to the boom-era level of prosperity. The underpinnings of this defective theory lay behind the aim of the near-trillion dollar stimulus bill passed by the US Congress in 2009 (the American Recovery and Reinvestment Act).

Economic growth confers a social benefit. Abundance over austerity is the aspiration. But to investigate the logical failure of Keynesian economics in these efforts, we must correctly understand its theoretical objective—how and why economic growth occurs. We must also take a deeper look at its "multiplier effect" and how the Keynesian school of thought attempts to produce such an effect through government methods.

In the spirit of the Keynesian approach, let's work backwards a bit—beginning with the "how" of economic growth. Pretend for a moment that a company, we'll call it Company X, is doing rather well and decides of its own accord to build a bridge. What might happen? Company X may hire a contracting crew to begin construction, and in turn, the contractor buys materials like steel and perhaps heavy equipment, say a couple of lifting cranes. The equipment dealership increases its orders to meet the demand for the new cranes, and as such, the crane manufacturer may have to increase its production to fill the new orders. Furthermore, the crane manufacturer may also have to hire new employees to meet the increased production, and these newly hired employees spend their money on groceries, gasoline, automobiles—you get the picture. This whole hypothetical sequence of events began when Company X made its own decision—freely I might add—to build a new bridge. Thus, this isolated and private decision set everything else into motion. This is the multiplier effect.

But where does Company X acquire the capital to build its new bridge? The answer is from its savings! Company X must have capital resources to construct the bridge—and in order to accumulate capital, companies operating under the market economy must always first persuade others. Now the savings discussed can be in the form of other's savings, stemming from investors, reliable credit, or simply the company's own savings account. But these resources exist—they were developed over time, not created from thin air. But to keep things straightforward, we'll stick with plain money, representing real resources that have been voluntarily saved.

To build the new bridge, Company X saved its money. (Of course, for such a large financial undertaking, normally a company would also finance at least part of the incurred expenses with the help of a bank loan, but to avoid dragging in fractional-reserve banking, we will equate "savings" and "matched savings with a bank loan" as one and the same).

The "Why" behind Growth

Why would Company X want to spend its resources (money) to build a bridge, the action which started the entire multiplier effect? It could be for a laundry-list of reasons—perhaps the nearest bridge is 40 miles away, and with the new bridge, transportation costs are reduced. Maybe Company X can entice more customers by offering easier access to its location. There can be a an infinite variation, but a sound company, unable to externalize its cost on taxpayers or other property holders, will make its decisions based on a larger return from these reasons given. That is, the return on its investment. Under the market economy, this economic calculation is vital to determining profit and loss. Whether it's a new bridge, a fleet of trucks, or something as small as a new type-writer for the secretary, the product of the decision is not the real importance here—it is the logical process to reach that decision which is.

Unimpeded market conditions fortify this ability to accurately forecast consumer needs, while providing a private company the naturally strong incentive to produce pragmatic and wise assessments. Profits are chased, but decisions are calculated with more precision, taking into account more longer-term factors. The crux of the matter is that prudent decision-making is nurtured.

Let us assume the first "why" we mentioned, that our hypothetical Company X wants to build the bridge to reduce transportation costs associated with fuel. So before Company X decides to build, it will study the costs and benefits of such a project (its return on investment). Company X figures that the bridge will cost one million dollars to construct, and that once the bridge is built, Company X will save fifty dollars in gasoline every year from its use. How long 'till it breaks even (the company's return on investment)? After you do the math (it's something like 20,000 years), all other factors aside, no one in their right mind would risk financial ruin for a project like this. But if the fuel savings from the bridge's use were two million dollars a year, it may indeed be a worthwhile venture.

So we'll stick with the latter hypothetical figures, and subsequently, Company X determines the bridge is a great investment and decides to move forward. The prudence of forward-thinking does not end there. Company X then plans for the bridge's construction, and realizes they must make more detailed decisions. They may further decide to go with a more expensive material upfront, as it will reduce maintenance costs in the future. Additionally, they will likely select the most cost effective manner of completing the bridge project, as well as the most capable construction crew—since Company X wants the job done right the first time. Natural incentives provided by market economics cause more rational decisions like these to be made.

Now, the multiplier effect, in accordance with its name, keeps moving after the bridge is completed. Company X can now produce the same service for a cheaper price, hence the company is more competitive, and revenue levels begin to rise from the increased business (consumers also become "richer"). Company X may now figures they must hire more employees to effectively handle the increased business from the fuel savings.

Under unhampered market conditions, the multiplier effect is normally beneficial to all because of this reason: Company X made a "free and isolated" financial decision from its own savings. The bridge project was a success. Company X carefully weighed its return on investment, from its own property earnings, or from property it was liable for. But what if Company X would not have been so fiscally careful and deliberate? What if they had been careless and the bridge project, for one reason or another, caused them financial ruin? Just as their decision to build the bridge was by nature "free and isolated", so too is their financial failure. In other words, Company X's financial failure would be limited to themselves, and only extending to perhaps those who voluntarily chose to participate in the Company X construction project.

We have looked at the "why" and the "how" of economic growth—real economic growth that is—and in the same light, we have also observed the multiplier effect. Within the parameters of this abstract analogy, the "why" and the "how" of real growth can be summarized as this: Economic growth is the increase in *ability* to produce goods and services, and it is generated by the investment of real, preexisting savings to achieve a greater return on said investment in the future.

We have defined the "how" and the "why" of economic growth, and we have also identified the source of the so-called multiplier effect—Company X's decision to construct its bridge. Building upon this framework, we can further investigate the Keynesian theory of government-directed stimuli. For starters, let's replace Company X with the Federal Government. In order that "demand" be shoved to new heights (why demand is deemed to be too low is somewhat of a mystery), the Keynesian way of thinking is that the multiplier effect can be reproduced using government. This begs the question, what would happen if Company X was substituted with the Federal government? The substitution provides a night and day difference and it can be best explained using the following criteria. Of note, we must remember here that the bridge analogy can also be substituted with practically anything—but no matter the object of the analogy, it is only to serve the purpose of exposing the flaws within Keynesian economics.

Investment for a Reason

As we have seen, Company X invests its money based on a projected return. What does the government want in return? Usually it is some sort of feeling of prosperity, typically taking the visible shape of more employment through economic growth. One of the fundamental problems is that this economic growth is "an end in itself" and this end provides adverse-market incentives to all those involved.

The government forks the money over for construction of the bridge, but with the lack of long term purpose comes a break-down in accountability. Without market incentives—like bearing the full cost of lost savings—this alteration in behavior can be quite evident in a broad host of planning categories, such as location, materials, quality, construction personnel, etc. The government only wants to put people to work, in hopes of some stimulative policy goal. The objective is not the overall project, but merely the initiation of such a project. More consumption and spending is its very target. More work is its ambition. Thus, once the project is initiated, its objective is sealed. What happens next is usually someone else's problem. And of course, here is where politics come in to play. Will the government carefully select the right construction crew for the job? Perhaps a contractor is chosen who happens to be the nephew of the district congressman. True, nepotism takes place in the private market, but say Company X chooses a contractor based on this criterion—if said contractor overcharges Company X ten thousand dollars, the market naturally punishes Company X ten thousand dollars for its nepotism. But this deterrent is not naturally applied with government.

In addition to this, the government could be even more careless. It could choose over-expensive material, waste money on unnecessary "consultants", or the accountability could be so lax that safety standards are disregarded.[14] In an unconstrained market, natural incentives also exist to maintain safety. Notwithstanding moral reasons—if an employee or worker is hurt, it not only could mean a lawsuit, but it also damages the reputation of those participating in the project and potentially hinders future economic opportunities. All of these measures stem from forward thinking. Government always tends to be present oriented. Once the stimulus project is finally completed, what do you have? A bridge that more than likely, will not afford any effective increase in productive aptitude: A bridge to nowhere.

Consumption vs. Production

To elaborate on "investment for a reason", Keynesian theory also assumes that economic growth rests on increased consumption. This is perhaps the largest blunder held by the followers of the "Keynesian Revolution". Consumption means little when value is not produced in the market—to understand this, we can look at something called the "broken window

---

[14] Rothbard, Murray. *A History of Money and Banking in the United States: The Colonial Era to World War II.* Auburn, Ala.: Ludwig Von Mises Institute, 2005. p.143-144 Rothbard details how safety standards can become debased if and when these standards are set by government and not the market. Comparing the concept to the widespread pattern of bank reserves tending toward the minimum government requirement, safety standards will also tend to be met in this fashion—as companies must no longer take into account "safety" as a criterion in market competition. When the government sets the standard, such standards can often times fall below what the market would otherwise push.

fallacy", which was first made popular by Frederic Bastiat, a 19th century French economist and philosopher.[15]

Pretend a band of well-intentioned vandals choose to perform a certain public service. This gang of good Samaritans decides to create employment and "spur" the economy. These "philanthropists" walk down the main street of a small town and break every car windshield they come across. Assuming they are not arrested, after a few nights of this charity work, what may likely be the economic result? Jobs may indeed be "created", because all the broken windows will now need window repairmen. Perhaps security guards will be hired to prevent future vandalism, and maybe mechanics will be employed to install new security alarms around businesses in town. Did this grow the economy? Should the gang continue its charity work by setting buildings on fire?

Of course, we can see this does nothing to grow the economy. That is, not in a real way. It is quite evident the only certain result is the consumption of resources, i.e. breaking windows and disparaging private property. These destructive activities are not producing anything of value. In effect, this "charitable work" is eating up personal savings and forcing people to spend money they otherwise would not have to. Take the new security guards. If their employment prevents further vandalism, it may "seem" like a good investment—only the vandalism is "artificial"—giving rise to *malinvestment*, or investment based on illusory demand.

---

[15] Bastiat, Claude Frederic. *The Bastiat Collection*. Second ed. Auburn, Alabama: Ludwig Von Mises Institute, 2011. p. 2-4.

Now, what happens when all of a sudden this economic "charity" for the community ceases—the vandals suddenly stop smashing car windshields (i.e. the government ceases its creation of new money)? Since the vandalism ended, what happens to the security guards, the extra window repairmen, alarm mechanics, etc.? All the economic "growth" which occurred is realized to be unnecessary—the new workers will likely be laid off because their services are no longer needed. We can now see the demand for their employment services were merely "propped up" by the "artificial" action of smashing car windows. When this concept transpires through money-creation, distorting interest rates, the process becomes more concealed, and the detrimental consequences more severe.

Indeed, what has really transpired is malinvestment, or the misallocation of resources. This analogy is a crude example of government destruction, done in the name of economic growth. This destruction not only causes the unnecessary consumption of savings, but also the consumption of healthy future investments as well. In fact, society at large grew poorer during the boom, though what is often directly seen through destructive activities was an "increase" in economic activity. What is often not seen though is the continued dwindling of this hypothetical community's savings.

What's also often missed here is the shift from forward thinking to more present thinking. Less incentive to save may linger, even after the destructive activities cease, as people may choose to consume what they can in the present, for fear that the same destruction may befall them at some point in the future. Still to this day, it is hard to fathom how many believe that natural disasters or wars will bring about prosperity. This train-of-thought is less excusable because of the overt nature of the destruction, but as we will later discuss, the more covert ruin of savings via inflation acts in a similarly vicious manner.

Over-consumption is a primary effect felt and seen first from ever-larger government. The government cannot invest, it can only consume. This is because it never begins with real savings. Unlike Company X in the analogy, the government ultimately acquires its funds from force. Furthermore, because government stimulus policy rests on consumption, the funds being used for economic growth are taken first from market production. Just as in the broken window fallacy, the perception of economic growth is a mirage.

The source of market growth and artificial economic growth is what divorces Keynesian economics from logic. Under unhampered market conditions, the original source of the "multiplier effect" was a wealth generator (remember Company X and its own savings from the first analogy). Utilizing government, the origination of this multiplier effect is a wealth consumer. At any one time, resources for present use are finite. Hence, without production, consuming in the present must eventually cease. Once the consuming is halted, as it inevitably must be, markets have been altered and misaligned. Depending on the length and severity of this non-market consumption, this alteration can be extreme. Individuals have been deprived of real resources, and many find themselves in sudden economic hardships. One of the primary underlying differences between government fiscal stimulus, versus monetary government stimulus, is the hidden, obscure nature of the policy. Monetary stimulus is usually much more detrimental, because the severity of its harm is not noticed, and therefore, resistance is mooted while losses go unrealized for far greater lengths of time.

The foundation of Keynesian doctrine rests on a concept which is simply unsustainable. By definition, over consumption by government can only continue for so long (whether it be deficit spending, taxation, or money-printing). What form it takes can shape the length of time that such policies can persist—while also determining the unproductive versus counterproductive effect on the market economy.

However, the alteration of the market economy's structure is what shifts government consumption from one of an unproductive nature, to one of a more counterproductive nature. Once the government stimulus runs its course, thereby shifting the structure of production, the fallout from this intervention generally begins. The spending must cease, and the economic bust will finally surface, many times with violent swings and corrections.

In addition, if such government stimulus takes the shape of deficit spending, this policy can be transferred from one of fiscal means, to one of monetary means. Deficit spending may originate on government borrowing from true savings, but these savings likely dry up, forcing interest rates higher. With the central bank in play, government usually shifts harmful fiscal policy to monetary means. In effect, even the "containment" of government borrowing from the general public will usually lead to inflation.

This consumption called stimulus tends to cease abruptly—by defaults on government debt, credit contraction to stave off currency failure—or the ultimate conclusion of consumption, the complete collapse of the monetary unit's purchasing power. In this case of hyperinflation, the government spending does not have to necessarily stop per-se; however, purchasing power of the currency will be so thoroughly diminished, the economic effect will be the same (albeit the social effect is widely more dangerous).

In the final analysis, all of these negative and illogical effects of Keynesian public policies are far from isolated (as in our original analogy with Company X) and by consequence, their results touch every citizen, making their implications all the more disastrous. The nasty effects of the Keynesian program have only been briefly visited, but they are too apparent. In reality, there is no "multiplier effect". This term was hatched by the econometricians and the planners in the wake of Keynes' irrationality. There is only one "multiplier effect" and that is the accumulation of capital. But the Keynesian prescription reverses this trend of savings. It "de-civilizes" society. Under this intellectual cover however, the national government's increasing appetite for consumption in the present marches on, typically creating new money to do so. Directing and influencing this increased consumption is determined by the planners, and winners and losers are chosen by arbitrary force— all in the name of prosperity. Poverty is created from a previous state of affluence, but this is the price that is asked in order to place a completely fallacious theory into action.

Investment is not an end in itself, and therefore, employment and economic growth cannot be either. It is determined by the calculation of return and the prospects of sustaining this return. Spending and spending consumes resources and dries up the needed flow of savings. This leaves less incentive to invest productively with the savings that remain. Furthermore, the government consumption finds its way into financing all types of hopeless projects, only prolonging the waste. Keynesian practice supplies an overt action that is good for elected officials, and perhaps votes, but which is harmful to the citizens it supposedly aims to serve. To the contrary, "overconsumption" by private firms will cause privatized bankruptcy, limiting the pain to those participants involved. Overconsumption by government is unproductive, and usually counterproductive. It leads to public poverty, and expands the pain to those innocents who never participated in the process to begin with. Furthermore, government consumption, increasing as it may, tends to create conditions of increased present thinking, at the expense of the market's incentive to look ahead.

The Market Entrepreneur: A Derivative of Economic Calculation

Logical economic thought, on the rise throughout the 1920s, was rejected by the decade of the 1930s, a decade which brought the Great Depression and mass unemployment. Though Ludwig von Mises successfully predicted that the credit expansion of the 1920s would lead to a catastrophic discombobulating effect on market exchange and investment, centralized government's tendency to embrace crisis with interventionist "action" was all too telling. The acceptance of the Keynesian prescription was fully embraced, shoving out the thoughts of Mises, and dominating the intellectual arena of this era.[16] The aftermath of Keynes is still felt today.

Prior to this Keynesian pollution of logic, Mises had already published his treatise on the business cycle. In one of the more critical contributions to coherent economic thought, Ludwig Von Mises identified the causes of repeated economic booms and busts. In his 1912 publication, *The Theory of Money and Credit*, the pioneer of the *Austrian School of Economics* (named

---

[16] Mises, Ludwig Von. *The Causes of the Economic Crisis: And Other Essays before and after the Great Depression.* Ed. Percy L. Greaves. Auburn, Ala.: Ludwig Von Mises Institute, 2006. See Chapter 2, Mises' essay "Monetary Stabilization and Cyclical Policy", p. 53-153.

for Mises' native nation) attributed these market phenomena to the expansion of fractionalized bank credit unbacked by voluntary savings.[17] Building upon Mises' framework, Murray Rothbard later indicted state-sponsored central banking as the primary culprit to orchestrated and prolonged inflationary efforts.[18]

The work of both of these men profoundly absolved the free market from the speculative mania characterizing the boom and the mass unemployment and bankruptcy characterizing the inevitable (but necessary) bust. Their analysis not only laid the foundations of the Austrian School—but it was the first to fully highlight the chaotic fallout from the deviation of sound money. In short, the Austrian School has been the only economic source to properly conclude that booms and busts directly result from institutionalized fraud and theft. This is the analysis which has eluded not just the Keynesians of today, but the modern mainstream economics profession altogether.

Mises' *Theory* has still not gained its rightful place in economic circles, for it was this work which first shed light on the negative effects of monetary expansion in the 20th century. The brilliance of his work lies in his connection of "macro"

---

[17] Mises, *The Theory of Money and Credit*. p. 139. Mises explains that the increase in the stock of money provides a heightened command over goods and services for those individuals who receive the new money first, bidding up prices on the goods and services this new money is traded for.

[18] Rothbard, *What has Government done to Our Money?*. p.83-84. Rothbard writes that central banking removes critical checks on inflation. Even under a fractional-reserve legal system, individual banks must restrict their inflationary measures; else lose their "clientele" to another bank which will call for redemption in specie, i.e. hard money. Central banking permits all banks under its wing to expand inflation, without the fear of interbank competition, based in reliability.

aggregate effects to the cumulative "micro" actions of individuals. Mises' work was in many ways one of the first to offer an all-inclusive integration of the two together, linking the effects of widespread monetary inflation to the individual actions and time preferences of the market entrepreneur.[19]

Many have ignored this work, and some have repudiated it. Even those economists labeled as "free market" have often overlooked Mises efforts, for very few American college campuses offer insight to the Austrian explanation of the business cycle. To further comprehend the nature of the business cycle, and its impediments to social and economic progress, a quick review is in order. The "boom" period of the business cycle begins with the aforementioned expansion of credit. In today's economy, this monetary expansion is made possible by the forced-institutions of fiat currency, fractional-reserve banking, and the government's central bank. To "stimulate" investment, the Federal Reserve—our country's central bank—injects new reserves into its member banks, increasing the supply of "printed" capital throughout the banking system. Since capital now appears more abundant, the price of this watered down resource is cheapened. Interest rates begin to fall—albeit artificially—signaling entrepreneurs that more resources are available for long term investment.

---

[19] Hoppe, Hans-Hermann. *Democracy--The God That Failed: The Economics and Politics of Monarchy, Democracy and Natural Order*. New Brunswick, NJ: Transaction, 2001. Mises theory gave light to individual time preference and the market rate of interest early in the 20th century. But See Chapter 1 of Hoppe's *Democracy—the God that Failed*, for a brilliant expose on individual time preference, the accumulation of which forms the natural market rate of interest.

As a result, more projects begin in the present than what otherwise would. Originating with the banks, the new credit enters the economy through the loan market, and as it does, the prices of capital goods are bid-up. Resources—including labor—are stripped away from their former roles. However, because the additional resources to produce these new investments do not exist, they are unsustainable in the long run. Entrepreneurs have been "fooled"—but do not realize their error until the rate of credit expansion dwindles, permitting rising interest rates to reveal their mistakes.

Once this inevitably comes about, the "bust" period of the business cycle replaces the boom—and these built-up, unsustainable ventures must be liquidated, while remaining resources can be finally reallocated to places more urgently demanded by consumers. It is only after the bust period sets-in that these new investments are finally realized to be in fact, malinvestments.

It must be realized that the market entrepreneur emerges from trial and error. Those individuals who best serve the sovereign consumer are rewarded with profits and tend to command more capital; those who fail at forecasting consumer demand receive losses and their capital is ultimately relegated by the consumer into the hands of those who add more value. This ability to forecast stems, however from economic calculation—without which, the market forecaster becomes an aimless speculator. In other words, the entrepreneur is established on the market only from the growth of reliable economic calculation, and if this is removed, so too is the forecaster. No amount of entrepreneurial talent can overcome the cessation of the tools which give this talent life. Without reliable economic calculation, the entrepreneur's talent is rendered moot—his existence cannot precede the root which gives his ability meaning. Consequently, as methodical economic calculation deteriorates, so too does the preeminence of the market forecaster. It is foolhardy to believe that one's talent will carry-on if the origin which gives those talents meaning is demolished—yet this is what has come about through government decree and force.

In this way then, it is important to understand the character of the government's monetary expansion—coerced exchange through fraudulent "counterfeit". Economic calculation, the power base of the market entrepreneur, is a system only applicable in the sphere of voluntary exchanges. It is precisely this venue which gives it any meaning at all. A network of these voluntary exchanges develops after individual valuations "price" the consensual trades through a marketable commodity. It is this pricing mechanism and media of exchange which permits the sophisticated growth of (first) economic calculation and (second) the market entrepreneur.

Thinking and choosing—or as Mises cited, *purposeful action*—becomes calculable, but only inside the framework of voluntary exchange. Just as economic calculation is a prerequisite for the market entrepreneur—so too is voluntary trade for economic calculation.[20] Outside of this framework lies the realm of involuntary exchange, an impulsive area of human

---

[20] Mises, *Human Action*, p.11.

action that renders economic calculation moot. When exchange is compelled through force, economic calculation diminishes in value. Coercive force is far more difficult to be "advertised" or expressed in any meaningful way on the market, for the market is defined by a two-way process. Coercion then is inherently indifferent to this cooperation.

Generally, the actions of a criminal are violent or deceptive, and the many categories of involuntary exchange range from outright theft or fraud. These criminal concepts have public counterparts, or in essence, institutionalized taxation, regulation, or currency debasement. However, between outright theft and fraud, one major difference exists. The two criminal acts—be they actions from centralized government or private individuals, are separated by a degree of realization. As previously state, in the first case of theft, the victim more immediately realizes his loss. In the latter case of fraud, the victim does not. For example, if a man robs a bank at gun point, the banker recognizes his deprivation the moment this criminal action occurs. If a man deposits one million counterfeit dollars, in exchange for say gold bars, the same banker may not discover the dollars to be counterfeit until some point thereafter. This lapse of time then differentiates these two basic forms of economic criminal proceedings; theft is always more presently noticed, while fraud tends to be observed less immediately. When assessing the causes of the business cycle—the expansion of the money supply and the wide-spread effect upon economic calculation—this difference is important to distinguish.

But despite these variances, one common denominator is present throughout every forced exchange: The behavior of *unilateral action*. Under any circumstance involving coerced cooperation, this one-party behavior is necessarily present. In any voluntary exchange, purposeful action is required from at least two parties of individuals, the *producing* party and the *consuming* party. Because of this two-party nature, communication is a necessary ingredient. In fact, it is not only an ingredient to the exchange, but it is also a byproduct from the moment of exchange. Any action is first "checked" by the other party to exchange—so that the rate and degree of change in supply and demand will likely be less dramatic than a forced transaction. At the very least, this combined bilateral action is telegraphed through pricing, as the increased communication must be broadcast to more than one party.

But there is no two-party prerequisite for involuntary exchange. The consumer acts irrespective of producer input. Consumption that comes about from involuntary exchange is not contained by market forces, as its limits are based purely upon the arbitrary whims of the consumer (regardless of the producer's desire). Involuntary exchange is not restricted to the available and various factors of production, but only on the supply of resources at any given moment. Because of this, involuntary exchange is often sporadic and extreme. Though forced action itself generates interventionist fallout, communication is not an essential prerequisite or byproduct. This innate characteristic strips interacting individuals from more *uniform* and *instantaneous* methods to determine and convey knowledge.

The violent or compelled exchanges typically have ramifications that are later visible through market pricing signals, but on the whole, these events cannot be foreseen with a great degree of accuracy, nor can the market entrepreneur's talents "overcome" or "evolve" to foresee these effects. Involuntary exchange and the effects thereof cannot truly be accounted for ahead of time with any degree of precision—not until these consequences have been integrated and filtered throughout the rest of the market itself. This is not to say that market actors do not react to forced exchange, merely that because of their sporadic nature, the extent, scope, and timing of this force cannot be measured through economic calculation. The market can indeed "arm" itself to coercive criminal activity by private actors (such as heightened security investments)—but of course, market actors are impotent to institutionalized government coercion by which defense has been monopolized. As F.A. Hayek warned, "...the more the state plans, the more difficult planning becomes for the individual."[21]

For our purposes though, perhaps most telling is the common phenomena that occurs with intervention or the threat of intervention. Because of the uncertainty, markets tend to "freeze up"; producers quit producing. This paralysis is a symptom of the inability for market actors to forecast and calculate the effects of forced exchange. Commerce is hampered

---

[21] Hayek, Friedrich A. Von. *The Road to Serfdom: Text and Documents*. Ed. Bruce Caldwell. Vol. II. Chicago: University of Chicago, 2007. p.114.

precisely because market actors cannot adequately calculate the size and scope of interventionist policy. All other factors aside, uncertainly leads to decreased production or a lack of commerce activity. Quite simply, economic calculation in and of itself provides no means for the market to forecast relevant data about criminal or government action. Indeed, many have talked about "business uncertainty" caused by the regime at hand, and the world of economic intervention it has created—but regardless of how "predictable" the government's increase in power becomes, the rate and change of this intervention cannot be coherently seen by market actors.

Malinvestment and Public Counterfeit

In hindsight, the consequences of forced exchange can be deduced. Up until now, we have only examined in economic terms the inability of market actors to precisely foresee or calculate the effects of intervention. But in our examination of the Business Cycle, the Austrians cite one specific form of forced transfer in their analysis—one that has been lost in modern life by the erosion of logic. Government monetary expansion has the same effect as criminal counterfeiting. The government's increase in the supply of money creates new media of exchange— simply by decree. And thanks to legal tender laws and the Federal Government's monopoly of the mint—the market is left with no means to distinguish the "new" money from the "old"—or which money represents real resources and which does not. This also holds true in the case of inflation, or by definition, the increase in the supply of money. When our government increases the supply of money, it is simultaneously decreasing the value of every other dollar on the market; effectively stealing resources in the same manner a Ponzi-schemer seduces his "customers".

But despite this overt analogy, most entrepreneurs (and bankers for that matter) do not see the monetary expansion through artificially low interest rates in this light. As previously stated, fraud is a crime typically not recognized in the present. Only later, when the bust which leads to depression sets in, is the crime recognizable through the form of malinvestments.

Though we have already demonstrated to the contrary, let us assume that the market entrepreneur is correctly able to forecast the government's monetary expansion and calculate the extent and degree of the "printed" inflation in such a way as to correctly assess the market's natural interest rate—for if this were the case, the entrepreneur could now avoid the malinvestment. This however, is pure fantasy. To achieve artificially low interest rates, the government's central bank injects, or pledges to inject, "fresh" reserves into its member banks, giving this industry unproduced resources to utilize for their own purposes. As we see in the Austrian theory of the business cycle, generally these nonexistent—or we shall say counterfeit—resources first appear in the loan market, pyramiding their way through the financial sector. At this point, the government has already begun the stealing process, while all together authorizing these privileged institutions to profit from it.

The Market Entrepreneur: A Derivative of Economic Calculation

Let us look again to the individual transaction at the point of exchange. The banker now uses the "fake" resources in the form of a low-interest loan to the market entrepreneur—which the market entrepreneur accepts (remember our assumption: the entrepreneur has somehow been able to calculate the natural interest rate, which of course would be higher than the banker's rate). Any argument to the contrary is defeated the moment the entrepreneur accepts the loan—regardless of this market actor's correct calculation of the real interest rate. This becomes clearer by remembering what the loan represents—false capital, or at the very least, *diluted* capital, and this counterfeit still commands resources and redistributes income. Pretend the entrepreneur's loan is for $1 million at the artificially low-interest of 3%. Due to the central bank's monetary expansion, say only 80% of this loan represents saved resources from abstaining consumers; the other 20% consists of the government's counterfeiting. As soon as the entrepreneur utilizes this 20%, he is utilizing the monopoly-privilege passed down to him from the government through the satisfied and contented bank. This counterfeit permits the entrepreneur to draw away capital goods and labor—or anything else for that matter—from their more appropriate market allocations. The market entrepreneur accepting the low-interest loan may indeed calculate his investment to be profitable at the higher market rate—of say, 7%. It makes no difference that the entrepreneur integrated the natural rate of interest payments into his total profit and loss projections—by passing on the counterfeit, he has merely passed on the malinvestment to tertiary producers. The counterfeit weaves its way through the market irrespective of the initial entrepreneur's investment—distorting prices further and further from the original market point of entry.

Perhaps one would still argue that the market entrepreneur can ward off the malinvestment by simply not investing the entire low-interest loan. If the entrepreneur only utilizes a portion—say the 80% which represents real capital—the malinvestment is prevented. In theory, this is the only way the malinvestment would not surface on the market—but this hypothesis is wishful thinking, ignorant to reality. If all entrepreneurs accepting low-interest loans forecasted the government's coercive monetary expansion, correctly calculated the extent of the counterfeit, deduced the real market interest rate—and by doing so—*subtracted* the diluted capital from the total bank loan, malinvestment could be prevented. We have addressed the impossibility of the first few points—but let's examine the last.

Monopoly Privilege: Irresistible Temptation

The government's inflationary efforts confer monopoly-privilege to those individuals first empowered with the new credit expansion. Through the counterfeiting process of artificial bank hand-outs, initial individuals receiving this benefit command more resources than they otherwise would. If somehow these early loan-recipients calculated the correct interest rate into their investments, malinvestment is a thing of the past and with it, the Austrian Theory of the Business Cycle. With a firm understanding of human nature, this logic can be firmly rejected.

Sticking to our previous analogy, the market entrepreneur receives an artificially low-interest loan of $1 million: 80% capital resources, 20% printed money—at a government rate of interest of 3% (remember, the market rate is 7%, or $800,000 in real capital—both of which our entrepreneur has hypothetically correctly accounted for). To avoid ANY market malinvestment altogether, the entrepreneur must withhold the counterfeit portion of the loan.

It has already been shown that to utilize the counterfeit is to at best, pass along the malinvestment. But the prospects of the entrepreneur abstaining from the use of these artificial funds are no higher than the chances of the banker abstaining from providing the government-inflated loan in the first place. Anyone that argues the opposite completely ignores the other side of the exchange—from the perspective of the entrepreneur at the bank. Surely, if the market entrepreneur will differentiate the market interest from the government's rate of expansion—than the banking entrepreneur will as well. But this is not the case. If entrepreneurs can distinguish the real market rate of interest from the effects of the government's monetary expansion, why then does the banking entrepreneur fail to include this information or "excess rate cost" into the loan offer?

Of course there are many explanations, but without a doubt, one primary reason is conferred monopoly-privilege.

Theorizing that the market entrepreneur will not utilize the monopoly-privilege of "high-powered" money (assuming he recognizes the low-interest loan as such) is similar to making the same assessment of the banking entrepreneur. Of course, the very existence of fractional-reserve banking—protected by government—is evidence that the temptation to employ this privilege is just too great.

One further vital aspect to the entrepreneur's reception of the loan is the moment of acceptance. *Time preference* has been expounded upon by many Austrian thinkers as the individual's valuation of present consumption to future consumption—and the sum of these individual time preferences is reflected through the market's natural interest rate (it should be further noted that the widespread "macro" *mal*investment stems from the disturbance of this spatial time coordinator).

As any "101" level economic class conveys, market entrepreneurs prefer lower interest rate loans to those priced at a higher rate. This in and of itself offers us still more insight. Continuing to operate under the assumption that the market entrepreneur has somehow forecasted the exact rate of coerced monetary expansion, correctly guessed the natural rate of interest, and calculated accordingly, the moment in time the transaction occurs is indicative of the entrepreneur's preference to utilizing the counterfeit monopoly-privilege. By accepting the artificially low-interest loan in the present, he demonstrates his preference for the privilege the present loan affords. By indicating his present preference, he indicates his unwillingness to abstain—he fails to demonstrate "sacrifice" for the future. If he is unwilling to abstain from accepting the artificial loan, he is also not likely to abstain from employing the counterfeit monopoly-privilege the government-enabled loan provides.

In addition, any subsequent market entrepreneur who would choose to abstain from partaking in the privilege of artificially low-interest financing (or dedicating resources towards this end) would find themselves, in the short term, at a grave disadvantage—nearly "forced" to take part in the credit expansion or find themselves out of business, bidding for higher-priced capital goods with their pre-credit expansion resources.

The Austrian Theory of the Business Cycle is as important to understand today as ever. As we have reviewed, the faulty analysis of the business cycle theory really stems from conscious and unconscious ignorance to the great contributions from the Austrian School—most notably the work of Mises and Rothbard. The faulty analysis of the individual market actor—in relation to government monetary expansion—reveals a great danger in today's line-of-thinking. Opposing statements of "easing credit to ease our pain" run with the same belief that government taxation is merely passed on to the consumer, which is then passed on in higher wages, in some crazy circle ending with no one "paying" the tax. It is this concept, this flawed analysis, which not only presumes monetary intervention is at best "surmountable" by the market, and at worst "irrelevant" to market functioning, that can be taken by policy makers and other economists that increased government intervention—in totale—is harmless.

Moreover, if we are to ever restrict government action, we can no longer provide a licensed economic writ-of-intelligence for government officials—as giving up the principles of sound economics gives way to the menace that comes with such intellectual justifications. Looking ahead, the further study of the market entrepreneur, economic calculation, and the effects of monopoly-privilege are not only all vital to understanding the current business cycle, but also to better understand the growth of centralized government, as well as the mammoth growth of the service sector economy.

Part III

The Erosion of American Manufacturing

Money Creation and the Structure of Production

These domestic boom and bust cycles caused by the expansion of the money supply are actually only part of a much greater international boom cycle which is directly linked to the exportation of this US inflation. This is the greater boom which wraps the others experienced as of late, under its wing—a boom which has yet to see its inevitable, but certain bust. This "umbrella" dollar boom has not seen its inevitable bursting, in large part, because of the American fiat dollar's foreign reserve status and the inflation which this now dwindling status has not only enabled, but necessitated.

Few economists or politicians take the time to account for this—that the Goliath service-sector economy in the United States today is truly one colossal malinvestment. Just as artificially low-interest rates caused by the Fed's counterfeiting led to a glut of unwanted houses being built across the American continent, so too has the production of more and more dollars to meet foreign "reserves" led to a prolonged gorging of imported consumer goods. This binge of consumption could never take place without the coercive reserve status propping up the paper dollar (and thus "demanded" and then "printed") in world-wide circulation. At some point, this insatiable appetite of swapping printed dollars for seemingly cheap foreign goods will come to an end. Drawing from our initial analogy, warehouses empty of widgets will no longer suffice the growing trade deficits the American continent has accumulated.

World War II saw devastation of lives and resources, the likes of which the world had never previously witnessed. But with the pledge of American welfarism and the subsequent flooding of US dollars, European markets began to complete their reconstructive healing throughout the 1950s and '60s. The long years of war had ravaged European capital and savings, but on the backs of the American producer—indirectly and directly—production resumed. Only instead of an "apple-to-apple" approach, with gold denominated exchanges, European banks and nations in Asia—including the rebuilt and westernized nation of Japan—were placed on the dollar system (Note: In the aftermath of the war, many countries accepted dollars with arms wide-open, looking at the relative stability of dollar reserves as "free" capital). No longer was international trade seamlessly connected through gold; practically all industrial markets would now be denominated in dollars, promised to be "as good as gold".

As we have covered via domestic business cycle process, those who receive the government's new money first benefit most. And so just as the domestic boom and bust cycle begins by permitting those who first acquire the newly printed money command over more resources than they otherwise would, so does the printing of new dollars give the United States the privilege of commanding goods overseas our country could not in the absence of this dollar hegemony in world markets. This new international system of dollar reserves—the result of the Bretton-Woods agreement—was solidified just prior to the end of the Second World War.

In its wake, immense pressure was exerted on the need for new dollars in which to use as a base line for other world currencies, initially pegged to the dollar. Of course it was promised that dollars could be exchanged for gold at some future point, but notwithstanding government promises, this newfound monetary system required a drastic expansion of the American money supply. Coupled with growing Federal Government expenditures in Europe during the 1950s and 1960s, there seemingly began a great demand for American money. Some of this inflation was aimed at filling domestic and foreign banking coffers with dollars, others at financing military bases and the emerging American policy of nation building.

But a certainty in all of this was that bureaucrats received larger budgets and bankers received more deposits. The new age of Pax Americana institutionalized the phenomena of monetary expansion in the name of "currency strength". However, it is not the production of new fiat dollars which enabled American economic growth since the Second World War (for trading partners in Europe were now poorer from war). Conversely, these actions by Washington—along with the Federal Reserve—undermined the strength of the American dollar. Ultimately this course of raw money production placed the nation on the now all-too-real trajectory of pure consumption, a form of economic "growth" absent market-based productive energies.

After Bretton-Woods in 1944, things began to change substantially for the dollar. Transactions between various national fiat currencies began to run through the network of central banks. All other factors aside—since foreign exchanges were now denominated in terms of dollars and not gold, American goods were numerically higher in price vis-à-vis their foreign counterparts. When Japan traded with France, each nation would first acquire dollars—either dollars they currently hold in reserve, or dollars they exchange for their own national currency. With every foreign transaction creating a superficially forced "demand" for American dollars (even when there are no American goods involved in said transactions), US goods in the short-run tend to be artificially higher in price—creating an obvious government-created disadvantage for the American producer, both internally and externally.

Under this paradigm, manufactured goods within the United States are more expensive than their foreign counterparts. Foreigners must "pay" for not only the American-made product, but also the artificially-increased use of the American dollar's reserve status around the globe. In addition, domestic firms specializing in consumer goods began to utilize capital goods from foreign providers. For instance, Detroit automakers would tend to import foreign steel, instead of the more numerically expensive product from Pittsburgh. As we will discuss later, this peculiar, but devastating situation is not entirely unlike Great Britain's experiment between the years of 1920-1925, when Britain's export industry suffered severe losses because of artificial barriers placed over the pound-sterling.

Now this is not to say that ALL economic decisions to utilize foreign products in the place of domestic-made goods were calculated and made because of this American monetary policy. Some were likely done simply because of the natural course of Adam Smith's division of labor; others from artificially higher-cost of increased union labor; and also of course, the growth of government—especially increased costs through new taxes and regulation—fueled by this very inflation, has done its part as well. However, the dollar reserve system was a massive contributing factor in every exchange between the consumers of capital goods and their corresponding producers.

The initial surge of the global dollar, combined with the effects of the inflation which followed, slowly but surely created an artificial "trading block", which ultimately debilitated the American producer's sales revenue. Over time, American monetary domination around the globe has eroded internal domestic production, crowded out from the enlargement of the service-sector this increased consumption has brought about. Substituting dollars in world markets—unlinked from real savings or property—liquidated the American manufacturing sector.

The Chinese "Hand Outs"

Of course, the dollar's "good as gold" status is a laughing stock today, and the shaky Bretton-Woods agreement finally collapsed in 1971—and with it, the gold-exchange window. One hidden casualty is that *Made in the USA* is an extremely rare label these days. Many seem to complain about it, how we as Americans simply don't make anything; how we have lost our manufacturing base and how a once productive nation has turned into a giant consumer continent. Take a trip to the local Wal-Mart, turn over any item, and it likely reads "Made in China", or a number of other Far East nations—but the unstamped mark "Consumed in America" should be carried as well. This growing trend of foreign imports that have replaced American-made goods on the shelves of every domestic retail store is said to be the curse of our country. The curse's cause though has gone unrealized.

But many today—especially politicians—who typically are inclined to play on emotional myth, fail to see the underlying reason for this lack of domestic manufacturing. At best, you will hear something about taxes and regulations. At worst, corporate greed, outsourcing, or a lack of "protectionism" and steep tariffs are cited as the fundamental causes behind this phenomenon. "Buy American" seems to be the offered answer. If only people were more "patriotic", we could reverse this course. But how can Americans buy American if there is nothing made in America to begin with? And beyond this, the few goods that are still made here simply cannot be afforded by the vast majority of the shrinking middle class and growing poor.

Both political parties have demonized these foreign imports, and many times, the emotional rhetoric has most notably fallen on the Chinese—one of the largest exporters of goods and products to the American consumer. Therefore, it is namely the Chinese who have taken the brunt of this hostility, who supposedly continue to "rip us off" by slaving away at toil to ship us products and goods, yet somehow simultaneously stealing our jobs and our wealth. If we examine the cause of this problem—the bloated trade deficit with China, annually growing at hundreds of billions of dollars—we can also see that the reverse of this proposition is true. In a way, we are "ripping off" the Chinese. Why? Because we're their worst customer, we don't pay! To understand this, we must continue our examination of the American monetary policy of inflation. In doing so, we can understand the genuine answer to why the American economy, which now consists of the largest service-sector ever known to man, fails to produce and manufacture. Once this is realized, we will also be able to see another looming economic and social crisis just over our national horizon.

By far, the largest contributing factor to the trend of American production being displaced with foreign imports has little to do with the traditional emotional-plays offered by politicians. Our nation's lack of production simply stems from our nation's lack of "sound money", or hard money notes exchangeable for gold or silver. Inflation has led to this unproductive status, for foreigners ship us goods, and fiat money is printed-up to pay for them. Yes, we don't make anything in the United States because as of now, we simply don't "have to". After all, is it not easier to print money, rather than utilize hard work and labor, to produce something valued to exchange overseas?

This scenario has taken time to develop, but it can easily be seen through our country's growing trade deficit, which has reached unprecedented levels, and now runs annually into the hundreds of billions of dollars (meaning, Americans import far more goods and services than Americans export).

Part of the reason that this state-of-affairs has lasted so long is that the Chinese—as well as many other nations—have foolishly followed the American example of inflation, running their own printing presses to keep up their exports to the American consumer. For years, the Chinese "pegged" their own currency, the Yuan, to the US dollar. To keep this fixed exchange rate in place, the Chinese government had to print more money to compensate for the Federal Reserve's massive "counterfeiting" of American currency (otherwise, all other factors aside, the Yuan appreciates against the Dollar). A more mainstream opinion presumes that the Chinese deliberately maintain a "cheap currency" in order to ensure that the American consumer imports Chinese goods at the expense of remaining American manufacturers. But the reality is that the Chinese government acts in much the same manner as ours—

the Chinese regime has a natural incentive to finance its own government expenditures with inflation, and the dollar reserves provide an opportunity to continue this. Chinese debasement of its own currency hurts the Chinese producer, just as American inflation has hurt the American manufacturer. But given the special-privilege awarded the dollar, the inflationary process first originates in the United States. Of the two economies, the American suffers the most, as the Chinese still produce. The just produce for less, for many of their goods are traded for continually devalued dollars. The United States does not produce, it consumes the Chinese goods (and of course, goods from other nations, paid for with devalued dollars).

A clear-cut paradigm made popular by Peter Schiff, Chief Executive at Euro Pacific Capital, is an example of 4 men who reside on an island, three Asians and one American. Each man is assigned a job, one Asian catches the fish, the other chops firewood, and the third hunts for deer—while the American's job is to eat the meal at the end of the day. Many economists have looked at this real-world scenario and seemingly asserted that without the American, none of the Asians would have a job. All would be unemployed. But we can easily see through this fallacy; for without the American, the three Asians live better. At some point, the three Asians realize that their standard of living would skyrocket by getting rid of the idle, non-producing American.

In the meantime, these growing trade deficits have created a precarious predicament within China, for the Chinese inflation which has "played along" with this money-printing contest has come to a crux. The more Chinese money that has been created out of thin air, the more prices have grown in domestic China. More and more dollar reserves have been piled within the Asian continent for Chinese inflation to fabricate on top of. Over recent times, the Chinese money supply, along with prices in domestic China, have gone up many times over, so much so that the Chinese government—fearful of the growing price inflation— has now resorted to price controls, freezing electric rates and other commodity prices. Of course, this can never truly solve anything, as the root of their inflation problem is the massive increase in the amount of Chinese Yuan in circulation. But during this period in China, much of these newly printed Yuans have gone into funding factories and other capital projects, many of which are tailored towards maintaining the supply of goods being shipped off to the American consumer (in return for more "printed dollars"). This is not to mention, the Chinese have also "lent" much of their remaining savings and real capital to the United States Government, purchasing trillions of dollars of American government debt (the 800 billion dollar "Stimulus" bill in 2009 was primarily funded from borrowed Chinese capital). The Chinese are beginning to realize they are never getting paid back.

But much like our last housing boom in the United States, this artificial boom in China cannot go on forever. It must come to a halt, and we are seeing signs of this "bust" already. Interest rates in China are beginning to slowly creep up, and in order to reign in the ongoing inflation, the Chinese money supply is now starting to contract, albeit slowly. The Chinese are beginning to slow the rate of their own monetary expansion, and have been in the process to seemingly permit their own currency, the Yuan, to appreciate against the dollar.[22] Price inflation in China is becoming too much to bear. What this means for China is that inevitably, their bubble-like economy will come to an end, and a recession in China will finally set in. This will indeed be painful for China in the short-run, but for the Chinese consumer, things will eventually become more affordable (because all of their countries goods are not being "freely" shipped off to the United States).

But what does this mean for the American economy? In the long term Chinese imports will likely dry up, or at least, drastically rise in price in terms of dollars—and since the American economy has transformed itself into one mammoth service-sector industry of banks, shopping malls, retail stores, hospitals, lawyers and tax accountants—we simply cannot supply the production void that will be left. Of course, other countries may try to do this for us, but there will still remain a far greater "lack" of use for US dollars on the international scene, once dollars become valued less and less. By letting their currency appreciate, the Chinese are also indicating that they will no longer blindly accept a continuous supply of counterfeit dollars for their own exports.

Yet the production of fiat money in the United States has reached new heights. Since the financial collapse of 2008—which in itself was caused by the expansion of our own money

---

[22] Kelly, Kel. "The China Bust: Tic Toc." *Ludwig Von Mises Institute.* Mises Institute, 10 Oct. 2011. Web. <http://mises.org/daily/5701>.

supply—our nation has readily increased the money supply of dollars at a more rapid pace. Whether it was bailing out banks, large corporations, labor unions, or providing currency swaps and "unlimited" dollar loans to the faltering Europeans, the United States government has desperately thrown itself down the age-old path of printing our way out of trouble, hoping to somehow regain prosperity and the ever-lasting economic boom. How naïve we have become.

More than likely, the faltering of the Chinese economy will set into motion a new American financial crisis—especially when China, along with other foreign nations, begin to sell off their dollar reserves and cease the new purchases of our debt via treasury bonds. When this happens, all of these new dollars that have created by the Fed over the years will finally rush home, not only pushing prices up, but perhaps causing a wave of inflation that could lead to dire economic and social circumstances in the United States.

In the future, Wall Street will have to become much smaller. If the American economy is to maintain one that is based on the private ownership of the means of production, more factories are needed in this country, not more banks. But for this to occur, Washington D.C. will have to become much smaller first. This path will come voluntarily or involuntarily, for markets in the end are always stronger than government fiat. To cure this disease though and follow a more fundamental economic footing, the United States government must discontinue the price-fixing of interest rates, cease the national printing press by dissolving the Federal Reserve, and permit market forces to regulate banks, fully legalizing the circulation of precious metals in trade and exchange. Better to take action now under more favorable terms, than wait until the market forces its own.

Redistribution by the Printing Press: The Heartland to Wall Street and Washington

Industry in the United States has been reduced to rubble-like levels, but there remains an intellectual shortfall, or a lack of a comprehensive account as to why, in particular, the manufacturing base which once flourished has "gone with the wind". Taxes and regulations, the overt impediments which can be seen with the naked eye, only provide a partial explanation. In spite of these steep taxes, banking has still pushed on to be as profitable as ever, even under the immense federal regulatory apparatus. Inflation has likely never been exposed as the underlying vehicle to this decline in manufacturing because it is largely a covert party to the dwindling capital stock of the country. But nonetheless, many manufacturing enterprises, if pursued in the United States, could not profit even if they paid zero taxes. Regulations on labor markets, entrenched in unionism, do offer some rationale. It must be remembered though that nearly half of US state governments have passed right-to-work laws, protecting voluntary contract from the infringement of forced unionism.

Still, the trend of the decline in manufacturing continues, and with some exceptions, many of the geographic areas that have become most "business friendly" have done so only to see retail malls and the service sector displace what used to be heavy industrial parks. In many different industries which once thrived a few decades ago, the final gross sales for manufactured goods would still be unprofitable—as domestic markets are saturated with debt, and export markets, denominated in dollars, are narrow and niche (Of note, the combination of high taxation and regulation typically falls harder at first on smaller, less established firms). Over-taxation and over-regulation is more of a side effect from inflation, rather than a true catalyst behind this lack of production, for this centralized control by government must be enforced with a vast bureaucracy. Inflation provides the growth of this apparatus, and as new money creation goes towards financing government bureaus in Washington, it eventually pushes prices and wages up throughout the rest of the market economy. These numerically higher prices tend to "bump up" wage-earners into higher progressive tax brackets, providing increased real tax revenues to the government.

As we have already revealed, the most significant contribution to the relative degeneration of American manufacturing has been inflation. Only by looking at the monetary policy of inflation in the United States can we also understand why those regions least connected with the established banking sectors have fallen to the severe levels of poverty today. Through a combination of government central banking, and a world-wide dollar reserve system, the US Congress and its sister cohort, the Federal Reserve, have systematically wiped out the country's manufacturing base, degrading the domestic production of capital goods within heartland of the country. Inflation, properly defined as the increase in the supply of money, has propped up over-consumption by continuing to erode the level of real savings left in the market economy.

To understand this process, and how this has come to be, one only has to imagine an organization that has been granted the exclusive legal privilege to counterfeit. This special "right" has long belonged to the Federal Reserve, which can create money out of thin air and pass this new money to its wide list of connected banks within its select member circle. And with its ability to "purchase" government bonds, there is seemingly no limit to the amount of revenue the Federal Government can blow through, regardless of how many taxes it can directly take in. This legal monopoly of the printing press tends to escalate in use, and like all government concentrations of power, it is often high-jacked by special interest groups. A counterfeiting ring has long been established, as friends of the counterfeiter line up to gain access to the injections of fresh cash. In fact, the only thing the Fed can do is turn to the printing press, for this has been the reason for its existence in the first place—to become the "lender of last resort".

Since the gold standard's final eradication, the purposeful increase in the supply of money has been very detrimental to the nation, but perhaps more so to the Midwest regions of the country—the areas furthest from the coastal banking powerhouses—which have long specialized in the manufacturing of capital goods.

By the 1970s, large manufacturing businesses had long been developed within Ohio, West Virginia, Kentucky, Pennsylvania, Michigan, and upstate New York. Over the course of the 20th Century, this heavy industry increased in productive output and employment. Between the early 1900's and the 1960s, a substantial portion of all commerce within these areas was based on the production of capital goods, or as discussed, goods which are not immediately used by the end consumer. The production of steel may be used to later make automobiles, the production of glass for windows, chemicals for plastic, and so forth. Because of the large presence of natural resources, like coal and timber, the crucial elements of the original factors of production—*both labor AND capital*—began to collide in the Midwest, and ultimately, these resources were developed into more valuable goods for the consumer.

Over time, these large investments produced wide varieties of capital goods such as steel, chemicals, glass, pottery, furniture, plastics, forged metals, and many others. The increased production paid enormous dividends, as the investments in productivity became ever more profitable, and the entire population was nurtured from this amplified income. In general, all individuals taking part of this concentration of capital benefited: Wages went up for labor, profit increased for business, shares paid more to stock holders, and prices fell for the consumer.

But the precursor to this accumulation of capital investment was one element absent in today's inflationary age of American money printing—***actual savings.*** The amount of savings, or the savings rate, is critical to lasting economic growth, and happens to be the key factor in determining an important "price" in the market—the price of present goods versus future goods.

Through the natural formation of prices, markets determine what consumers want and what and how much should be produced. But prices do not just determine what and how, but also when. The "when" price is perhaps one of the most significant signals in the market economy— otherwise known as the interest rate. The rate of interest coordinates the proper relationship between production and consumption across the spectrum of time. When individuals decide to save, they abstain from consuming all of their income in the present. As a result, resources that are not immediately consumed begin to become more and more abundant, and the rate of interest on the market naturally falls in price. As the supply of these savings continues to grow, the price of investing in the expansion of capital goods becomes less and less expensive. These newly saved resources can be invested in further production, and in time, will yield an increase in the ability to produce greater returns in the future. Savers are the true "capitalists" in our society—as they provide entrepreneurs with the vital resources necessary to increase society's standard of living. Given the historic tradition of heavy industry in the Midwest, and its role in supplying capital goods to the nation (which always represent future goods, as capital goods are not immediately consumed), increased savings would only stand to further benefit our state, as more investment potential becomes available for the expansion of capital goods production.

However, when a country's government pursues the printing press (as the United States has), the real savings of its residents are severely reduced, and future goods become much more expensive in real terms. Our Federal Government's monetization of debt and its continual actions of "printing money" have reversed this natural process of saving that the market economy tends to bring about—instead of increased savings, savings plummet. In place of falling prices because of the continued increase in the development of resources, prices are expected to continually rise (as resources are diverted into government expenditures). Lastly, instead of further production and higher real wages—the reverse becomes true. These actions can also alter the "time-preference" of individuals, because by artificially pushing numeric interest rates down (by the Fed's expansion of the money supply), real resources become diluted—as the supply of newly "printed cash" gives the false appearance that capital has become more plentiful.

Real Income: The Service Sector vs. Manufacturing

Time preference is the orientation of the individual with respect to his inclination to consume now, or abstain for more in the future. The process of civilization is derived from the ability to postpone immediate consumption, with the expectation of receiving something more valuable in the future. Time preferences vary from one individual to the next, and can change many times over the course of a lifetime, and as stated, the rate of interest is determined by these collective individual valuations, the price between present goods and future goods. Individuals with lower time preferences, or those who sacrifice from present consumption in order to gain something of greater value in the future (i.e. savers), generally either provide the capital, or the foresight, to increase the economy's productive ability (i.e. the market entrepreneur). However, the market economy naturally brings about lower time preferences for all because as these savers escalate their ability to produce, the supply of goods and services are made more abundant. This rise in the provision of goods lowers the price per unit of good, thereby increasing the real incomes of others.[23]

Worth emphasizing is the fundamental difference between capital and consumer goods. As mentioned earlier, consumer goods are those goods produced for more immediate use, while capital goods are those goods produced, not for an end in themselves, but in order to achieve a later end. Capital goods are used to produce other goods for consumption at some point in the future. For example, pretend a man is stranded on an island. In order to survive, he must catch fish from the shoreline. Rather than catch fish by hand—a time consuming and less productive action—he figures that he can drastically increase his productive efforts if he builds a fishing net from the various materials on the island. He calculates that it will take three days to find enough material and furnish the finished net. But what will he eat while he is building his fishing net? He must first abstain from eating all the fish he catches by hand, placing some aside for future consumption, to provide for his meals during the three days of fishing net construction. He must save, and after the three days, his fishing net allows him to use far less energy to catch far more fish. Under these conditions, we can see that the fish is the consumer good, and the fishing net is the capital good, or the good used to produce other goods for consumption.

With this in mind, the complex economy has a sort of chain of events that occurs before consumer goods are finally delivered to completion. Each stage of production can be

---

[23] Hoppe, *Democracy—The God that Failed*, p.10.

described as more fitting towards the capital goods category, or closer to the consumer goods category, depending on how far or how close these goods fall within the various stages of production from the end consumer. A capital good then is really nothing more than a good that is valued by someone for the sole purpose of completing a given task in the future. It is removed farther in the productive process from the production of the finished consumer good.

This example can also show us that some individuals have lower time preferences than others. For instance, some men stranded on the same island may never have the foresight to build a fishing net. Or in their view, perhaps the sacrifice of putting enough fish away to build one is not worth it. For others, their individual circumstances may require more than three days to construct such a fishing net, and therefore the task is not an option. Or they may not be able to accurately forecast how much time such a task will take, and do not wish to risk the potential loss if their calculations prove wrong (if the action is commenced, and the fishing net is found to take six days, rather than say the three days originally calculated, the man would go hungry, as his savings was not ample enough to sustain him through the entire process).[24]

We can see here than the man with the lower time preference initiates the stages of production farthest from the

[24] De Soto, Jesus Huerta. *Money, Bank Credit, and Economic Cycles*, p.274-280. To simplify time-preference and economic calculation, De Soto cites and elaborates on the example first given by the 19th century economist Eugen Bohm-Bawerk—of Robinson Crusoe on his island, engaging in more "capital intense" productive activities by developing a tool to pick berries more efficiently.

consumer, sacrificing present consumption and taking a calculated risk to construct his net. Once this net is completed, even others with higher time preferences will eventually begin to benefit, as the man with the fishing net can produce more fish than what he can likely eat himself. He can trade his spare time or excess fish with others, show them how to build a net, or just establish the simple example that it can be done.

Under the complex market economy, many choose to trade their own labor in exchange for immediate consumption, i.e. employees. The employer in essence, abstains from immediate consumption, in order to receive greater returns in the future. The income given to these employees is ultimately determined by the supply of real capital at their employer's hands.

Going back to our example, imagine another isolated scenario where individuals on the island are hired to work for one of the various producers. Suppose that one "employer", who catches fish by hand, becomes skilled enough at his fish-catching that he can hire another to cook his fish for dinner. Now imagine in a different setting that another man, the one who has saved and furnished himself with a fishing net, decides to hire a cook as well. Which cook will likely receive more fish for himself at the end of the day? One producer is by far more productive—he can catch 200 fish every day in the market instead of 2—and hence, obtains more resources. All other factors aside, it is likely that the cook who is employed by the man with the fishing-net will receive more fish to eat after the meal is cooked. This is why employees who work for those with capital goods—and in the capital goods industry—generally receive more income than those who work in the consumer goods industry. Regardless of the employee's general skill level, the cook who works for the man with no fishing net—who despite being the best cook on the planet—will never receive more fish at the end of the day than the cook employed by the man with the net. In other words, a janitor at Burger King will likely never earn as much as a janitor at a car factory.

Now enter inflation, which always tends to first burden those in the capital goods industry—the industries which typically provide greater income for those employed. The underlying cause is much the same as the reasons we previously explored for why the capital goods industry suffers from malinvestment and unemployment during the business cycle. This is because economic calculation becomes ever more critical to those industries within productive stages furthest from the end consumer.

Fishing nets eventually need replaced, so the producer on the island with a fishing net must always calculate when he will repair his net after it becomes less useable through depreciation. He must again set aside savings for this "down time" from fish catching, the time that he must instead dedicate to mending and tending the upkeep of his fishing net.

Since we have already discovered that inflation greatly distorts economic calculation (by increasing the supply of units by which this calculation is performed), the negative consequences will first be seen in the capital goods industry (the man who has no fishing net, who catches fish simply by hand, who deals strictly in consumer goods, does not need to calculate time spent away from catching fish). Inflation then gives the appearance that far less time is needed for the maintenance and replenishment of capital goods, at least at first.

Imagine that some of the fish the man with the net catches are inedible, they are rotten, yet since this has never happened before, the producer will not find this fact out until later on at some point in the future. Because of this, he will not be able to eat all the fish he catches. But since this is not immediately realized, the man with the fishing net still "logs" the same amount of time needed to repair his fishing net. He still calculates that it will only take him 2 days to perform the upkeep to his net, because he still believes that he has enough fish saved from his current batch to hold him over during this time period. The fact that some of the fish are rotten is only be revealed to him after he begins his downtime maintenance on his fishing net, and realizes that he cannot consume part of the fish he had placed away into savings. He then takes "losses"—as he did not necessarily midjudge the amount of time taken, but rather the amount of real resources at his disposal. He must either go hungry for part of this time, or ditch the unrepaired net to catch fish by hand again in hopes of getting an immediate meal. But of course, he is not the only one affected by this distortion in calculation. His cook will be left with less income as well. As the fishing net was never repaired, less fish can now be caught and cooked.

Inflation can be seen as the rotten fish. It dilutes the money supply, the commodity that provides for economic calculation, and silently dwindles the capital stock of the producer, falling harder at first on those industries most dependent on accurate forecasts. It holds true that the first sector of the economy to be negatively affected by this inflationary policy is typically the sector which produces capital goods—industry and manufacturing—which must be able to utilize accurate accounting. Up until the 1970s, manufacturing was progressing in a healthy manner inside within the United States. Notwithstanding the boom and bust cycle, which inevitably comes about because of this "cheap money" policy of mal-investments (the NASDAQ bubble, the Housing boom, etc), this longer-term phenomena of a diminishing capital stock has been brought about because of this inflationary age.

Since this deviation from the course of sound money, we can see the fallout. Real savings continue to become diluted and the production of capital goods becomes increasingly realized to be too expensive and too unprofitable to undergo (in 2005, the real savings rate in the United States actually dipped into the negative). As printed "credit" continues its havoc throughout the domestic economy, the trend of inflated government deficits, a larger and larger propped-up banking sector, and the fueling of over-consumption and a bloated service-sector has become the norm. Real wages and income for all left in the private market is reduced, but heaviest hit are those in the capital goods sector, who are forced out of business or employment.

With the gargantuan artificial service-sector crowding out the manufacturing base—by way of the extended, time-consuming currency devaluation—one can see that some groups benefit at the expense of others, while real savings are depleted on the whole. Even with workers making the shift to fill new jobs in the service sector, their real incomes will be lower distributing consumer goods rather than producing capital goods.

This inflation though has been prolonged because of other factors. Isolated under domestic conditions, and unable to externalize this cost onto foreigners, prices on end consumer goods would have sky-rocketed by now. However, foreigners have long been "hooked" and pressured, politically and militarily, on the American dollar—to both hold as reserves in their banks and to denominate with when trading in critically demanded global commodities. Long ago, the US government slowly forced a dollar monopoly on the rest of the world, and thus, even after the last gold window was closed in 1971, sovereign nations abroad were "talked into" exchanging various commodities first (or only) in dollars, while their central banks utilized our currency as reserves to pyramid their own inflation over.

The most notable of these dollar traded commodities has been oil, and the "petro-dollar" has thereby helped to prop-up our national currency, delaying the inevitable result of any governmental paper standard. Regardless of these temporary measures to stave off collapse, domestic production of capital goods has ceased to become "worth it", for no one can produce the effort to manufacture and industrialize in an economy that can simply print money out of thin air, and give to foreigners to labor and sweat for them.

The United States has largely become an island of consumption, whereby production is a thing of the past. This system benefits those who receive the new inflation first, while destroying those who receive it last. The belief that "Made in the USA" has gone by the wayside because of free trade is grossly misguided. There is only "one way" trade, and this can be seen quite readily by viewing the annual American trade deficits, fast accumulating into the hundreds of billions of paper dollars.

Overall, this massive redistribution of income—at the hands of our own national government's policy—has continually robbed manufacturing production domestically by fraudulently concealing the theft, but all the same, directing these seized resources into more and more service consumption. Though it has taken time, the result has been the utter liquidation of the heartland's industrial economy. Forty years of inflation and printing money has truly been the rain that brought about today's rust belt. It should be no surprise then that for some time now, two of the largest employers outside of the coastal financial conglomerates have been government and Wal-Mart.

The Inflation Tax and the Myth of Export Stimulus

Under cover from Keynesian intellectuals, economic fallacies continue, even in this age of widespread ease of information. Much of the time, media headlines report statistics, economic statistics which for one, are typically issued by government bureaus, and two, are meaningless if one cannot place them into context. Gross Domestic Product (GDP) is often cited as the statistic which indicates recession or prosperity, for as long as this remains a positive number, then supposedly economic growth is also "positive". Tallies like this statistic, which merely adds gross private spending with gross government spending, does not necessitate fundamental economic well-being. This measurement used to gauge the country's growth only takes into account "end" spending. As mentioned, this number placed on total spending levels is tallied up by combining private sector consumption with the total levels of government spending. While this measurement would certainly show an increase—because of the massive amounts of government money, borrowed from foreigners or monetized out of thin air—the structure of the economy has been significantly altered.

Since government action always and everywhere must first consume resources forcefully from other producers, it should come as no surprise that the GDP number—bloated by massive government spending actions—may not reveal the patient's ailment. For if the government tomorrow printed trillions of "surplus" dollars and handed them out, GDP would certainly be positive in the short-run. GDP more accurately represents gross consumption and if used to measure prosperity, it is often times misleading. By only measuring gross consumption, this statistic can never convey other significant economic factors. In the long term however, it is critical to analyze the real effects this goliath-dumping of government money has caused on the actual productive structure of the domestic economy.

For starters, this Federal Government money has certainly provided perks for those interest groups closest to government. Government contractors, bureaucrats, and other government-associated enterprises benefit with this huge shot-in-the-arm advantage. The increased levels of government-spending have given these special-interest groups more and more power to command resources than what they otherwise would have had, helping these politically-connected groups to bid away raw materials and other resources from the true private sector firms in the market economy.

The influx of government money from Washington D.C. on the rest of the nation has also had the effect of raising the price on goods and services for private industry and the like. This is in some way, an additional "tax", as these private firms and companies must now pay higher prices for these raw materials than what they did before— and higher prices for the same amount of goods and services. This forces private sector firms to become stretched thin, and the burden for smaller businesses can become just too much.

To illustrate this concept, imagine a small construction company, which primarily makes its money by building residential houses. Before the enormous amount of government fiscal "stimulus" was allocated, prices were fairly steady for the raw material this small company purchased, in order to build its homes for its customers. Once the "stimulus" money came roaring in however, politically-connected businessmen were awarded the funds, and new, often times "made-up" government work was dished-out. For example, these specially-privileged contractors began to build new public buildings, re-pave roads, or place another layer or two of paint on government-owned bridges. Concrete, asphalt, paint, equipment, and a whole host of other construction materials began to increase in price—or at least remain higher in price then what they would have been otherwise—as these materials are now in heavier demand throughout our local economy. To continue building houses for their customers, the small construction outfit must now pay these higher prices to continue its own production. These higher prices effectively represent a new tax on "the small guy"—or the individuals that do not receive the government money first, the guy who remains in what is left of the "free economy". The crony capitalist wins, and of course, the true capitalist loses.

Quite telling that this concept has indeed taken effect is the fact that over the last few years, the growth of private sector firms has been virtually non-existent in the Midwestern United States. Since 2009, some statistics show that private sector growth in this region has actually been negative. Government spending "crowds out" the private sector, as they both must compete for the same amount of scarce resources. Since government can naturally confiscate more money—without having to voluntarily persuade others that these new projects are both necessary and useful—the government typically comes away as the winner.

But perhaps one of the biggest myths that is still propped-up by the Keynesian intellectuals has been the fallacy that a cheap currency actually helps manufacturers and other exporters. This mythological belief—that debasing the dollar benefits exporters—is widely accepted by businessmen and the media alike. After all, more foreigners seemingly demand more export products if our money is "worthless". But upon closer examination, we can see how flawed this phony idea truly is.

The export sector began to seemingly surge shortly after the Federal Government—with the help of the Federal Reserve Banking System—began to severely debase and devalue the US Dollar, not long after the financial collapse in 2008. In an effort to boost liquidity, provide monetary stimulus, and help exports (all phrases used as a pseudonym for printing more and more money), the Fed has essentially engaged in outright money printing, "counterfeiting" hundreds of billions of US dollars since 2009. But since then, exporters in the United States have seen their product demand overseas grow substantially. This increase in export shipments however did not come from new *real* demand for the exported product or from an increase in domestic productivity, but because foreigners could now "make out" by buying these export products at the same *numeric* price, only with a less-valued US dollar. This happened across the board in American export markets, not just those located within the Midwest or the "heartland", but since most remaining American industry still lies within this region, it was the most affected.

This surge in exports though is merely an sort of accounting illusion, as these export companies—such as those in manufacturing—are actually selling their product to foreigners in return for *less* real resources than what they otherwise would have before the government "money-printing" intervention took place. In fact, these exporters are taking losses, but do not yet realize these shipments as losses until later, after the new money created forces prices on materials, goods, and services higher and higher (Depreciation costs will be higher than accounted for, if they overtly realize the losses at all). In essence, exporters are moving more product, but they are moving more product for less in return. All the worse, because this fact remains hidden until the harm is already done. Like the man with the fishing net who does not realize his fish are rotten, the harm comes later, once real resources are finally known to be less available (typically when the purchasing power of the currency is further depleted).

These direct federal subsidies also have another tertiary effect—they make state legislators in the various states more insensitive to the real consequences of direct over-taxation. When the government consumes more and more wealth from society, private individuals must produce with less, typically leading to less tax revenue in the long run. But since the federal transfer payments plug these shortfalls, the cost of state governments direct taxation becomes concealed—this effect of less and less revenue becomes hidden to the eyes of those in power, as numeric sales of exporters within these various states have increased on paper.

Currently, state and local governments are collecting tax revenue from this artificial-economic growth: artificial because this government-funded GDP growth is simply not sustainable. It will eventually cease to exist, as consumption cannot be sustained without the underpinnings of productive energies. With this illusory tax revenue being generated from the mammoth federal deficit spending, new government programs at all levels have been implemented—expanding the reach of government enterprise even more. Over the past few years, as the private sector has struggled to keep its head above water, the budgets of many state governments have exploded. Of course, the increased amount of state tax dollars coming in is partly caused by the increased federal spending. All of this spending and consumption continues to grant the appearance that both government and the private economy can be "big" at the same time, or that somehow, in defiance of economic law, resources are no longer scarce.

Part IV

Foreign Intervention

The Link between Empire and Inflation

Like other forms of government intervention, the money supply is by far no exception. As we have discussed, above all else, centralized government tends to target the money supply for control. This has been the history of American monetary policy—an unfortunate development that such a public policy of counterfeiting exists to debate in the first place. Once government high-jacks the money supply, as has been the slow but steady case via central banking and fiat currency, government can pay for activities it otherwise could not—with minimal revolt from the public in the short run. Financing government enterprise via inflation delays the day of reckoning. The higher prices that are sure to follow are put off until tomorrow and the day after, and the sour economy, along with the inflationary storm that comes can typically be blamed on something other than the true cause, such as profiteers, greedy capitalists, price gougers, or cheating foreigners.

Of course, we have examined the domestic government policy of "free money", one that has wrecked our national economy. Politicians continue to buy votes through the welfare and entitlement state, and of course, much of the time, use the printing press to fund these giveaways. This has also led to a massive phenomenon of increased present consumption at the expense of savings and manufacturing. But as of yet we have not examined another key factor, one that is pivotal both as a cause and effect of American inflation. Looking outside our borders at American foreign policy is also important to understand our unproductive service-based economy.

Empire and bankers go hand-in-hand. This is because they have a very sinister friend in common, that of inflation. Empire entails foreign conflict and the initiation of wars abroad— and as all veterans know, these wars are not cheap. They are paid from the public treasury—and the blood of human beings. Economically though, people generally dislike paying for wars that are not clearly aimed at their own defense. In other words, the individual prefers a return on their investment. Spending funds on security is quite different than spending funds on futile foreign and belligerent wars.

To circumvent this pesky obstacle of resistance though, governments have typically financed wars of aggression via debasing the currency. For instance, many of the European powers paid for World War I via inflation, just as the United States financed much of the Vietnam conflict by printing more dollars.[25] This behavior appears over and over again throughout a multitude of wars during the 20th century.

Many modern day economists overlook the effects of wartime spending on the health of the economy. Turning to Mises:

---

[25] Herring, George C. *America's Longest War: The United States and Vietnam, 1950-1975.* Fourth ed. New York: McGraw-Hill, 2002. p. 245-247.

In every great war, monetary calculation was disrupted by inflation...the economic behavior of the belligerents was thereby led astray; the true consequences of their war were removed from their view. One can say without exaggeration that inflation is an indispensable means of militarism. Without it, the repercussions of war on welfare become obvious much more quickly and penetratingly; war weariness would set in much earlier.[26]

At some point though, inflation becomes more evident, especially as foreign imported goods become more expensive when denominated in the domestic currency being devalued. Without a biased nationalized mindset, when one looks upon the spread of the American military dominion around the globe, more and more government control of the American money supply can be readily revealed. A huge point overlooked by the historical record is that American imperialism was not merely military, but monetary—for foreigners must be "kept in line" if they are to continually accept devalued US money for their goods.[27] This is an important concept to place into

---

[26] Mises, Ludwig Von. *Nation, State and Economy: Contributions to the Politics and History of Our Time.* Leland B. Yeager, trans. New York: New York University Press, 1983. p.163. Cited from Joseph Salerno, Ch. 19, "War and the Money Machine: Concealing the Cost of War Beneath the Veil of Inflation", Denson, John V. *The Costs of War: America's Pyrrhic Victories.* New Brunswick, N.J.: Transaction, 1999. p.433.

[27] Rothbard, Murray. *A History of Money and Banking in the United States: The Colonial Era to World War II.* Auburn, Ala.: Ludwig Von Mises Institute, 2005. p. 218-234. Rothbard details the origins of the gold-exchange standard, the basis for the British pound system in the 1920s, but more importantly, the American-dominated Bretton-Woods agreement after World War II. Replacing silver or gold "hard money" standards in foreign nations with a "dollar as good as gold" permitted US monetary policy to inflate dollars without the threat of a foreign run on gold. This technique was first implemented by the United States in the wake of the Spanish-American War.

context, because as dollars become devalued, controlling foreign acceptance of this inflation is crucial in keeping it going.

By the end of the 1800s, the War Between the States was over, and the Federal Government had consolidated its position, putting an end to the sovereignty of the states, the last substantial check over centralized authority. The road to nationalization had started. The free market was on its way out, and in its place arose the steady onslaught of government-assisted cartels. The terms Big Business and Big Labor were coined during this age of progressive national government. With the largess of the national government came an ever increasing standing army, the kind Jefferson and Washington alike warned against. Once the enormity of the military becomes institutionalized, government leaders tend to use it. It becomes a resource to utilize once in power, and the temptation has become difficult to resist.

On the back of Abraham Lincoln's military state, the Spanish-American War presented a convenient conflict to escalate imperialist goals. But as it turned out, it was also an excellent opportunity for some to begin the path of monetary hegemony, for powerfully connected bankers in the country had received a taste for government-backed industry during the Civil War. Although originating perhaps with Alexander Hamilton's First National Bank, it was not until the post-antebellum period that this "banking lobby" began to push for a more permanent central banking establishment in the United States.

With the end of the Spanish-American War in 1898, the United States acquired many new foreign territories. The Pacific islands of the Philippines and Guam, as well as the Caribbean islands of Puerto Rico and part of Cuba now fell under US control. The US War Department, along with other federal agencies, sent their representatives to the newly occupied US territories, to, among other things, establish a more "sophisticated" currency and exchange model. It is here that the inauguration of what Murray Rothbard described as American "monetary imperialism" found its beginnings.

The newly devised system would not be a continuation of the classical gold standard, the uniform standard by which all goods and services can be exchanged at face value. The new plan was the start of our current system—coercing foreigners to use US dollars as their reserve. By ditching the classical gold standard in the newly occupied territories, the US would force these economies off their respective gold or silver standard and onto a "dollar standard". The catch to this was that the older domestic currencies would be "price-fixed" at a lower exchange rate to the US dollar, eliminating gold from the equation altogether. This use of political coercion permitted the dollar to command more goods and services in these economies than it otherwise would.

The US also compelled these territories to back their own currencies not with gold or silver, but merely with US dollars, all of which were now kept in politically connected banks in

New York.[28] Not only did this new monetary imperialism grant—through force—more customers for the big American financial houses, but it also permitted US bankers to steal de facto resources from these new depositors.

Now of course, with unnatural demand placed on dollars, American exports to these new territories would be artificially higher priced vis-à-vis competing exports denominated in other currencies. But the entire focus of imperialism is to expropriate from others, or to essentially steal from new foreign territories. The myth of "opening up markets" for US exporters is less than a truism—increased raw consumption has always been the aim. The Federal government's militarism, driven by the power of government-connected bankers and other special interest forces was an underlying key to these policies. This militarism takes massive government expenditure, and at the close of the Spanish-American war, the US had amassed a considerable amount of debt from the conflict, short-lived as it was. Overvaluing the US dollar relative to the local currencies in the new US territories permitted the Federal government to further loot the occupied islands. Some of the burden of our military expenditures would fall squarely on the newly formed governments in these territories—and though their former currencies were still legal tender for debts, the Federal Government's price fixing and overvaluation of the dollar meant that the balance of these expenditures would collect more resources than would a true market rate under the gold standard.

---

[28] Ibid, p.219.

In this way, any good or service denominated in the former territorial currency will not "cost" less for American occupiers using dollars with the new forced price-fixing exchange rate. Conversely, it was not that the American dollar was more valued by the individuals living in these territorial areas; it was only valued in this way through the US force of displacement, permitting American bankers and bureaucrats to expropriate wealth and resources.

For instance, after the war settled, the US silver dollar was introduced in Puerto Rico. The former Spanish colony's national currency at this time was the Puerto Rican silver peso, which was legal tender for all debts. American authorities quickly compelled the Puerto Ricans to exchange their old pesos for the new silver dollars, at an artificially low rate of 60 cents to the dollar.[29] Thus, more resources would be coercively taken from the Puerto Rican economy, simply by forcing this price-fixing scheme on the new American territory.

In addition, if US bankers inflated the amount of dollars in circulation, there would be no danger in losing gold to creditors residing within these new territories. Since the price between currencies was fixed, these territories would find that goods and services exchanged for dollars would be paid for with an ever-devalued US dollar. Perhaps this historical point is most important of all in the long run understanding of our epidemic inflation today. Coercing others to use government fiat paper allows more printing press payments from the government doing the coercing to begin with. But the islands of the

---

[29] Ibid, p.221.

Philippines, Guam, Puerto Rico, and Cuba were anything but mature economies during the early stages of the 20th Century. There was no market for American goods in these newly won territories, because their resources had not been developed yet. No market meant no real interest on behalf of American exporters to attempt to halt the imperialist agenda. In fact, the only thing US officials were interested in exporting was forced military occupation and inflation—both of which are achieved more easily by seizing wealth through the mechanism of currency fraud.

The Follies of British Monetary Coercion

This early example is important to understand, because although this first stage of American monetary domination during the Spanish-American War was somewhat minute, in terms of economic size and scope, these same corrupt monetary concepts that benefit war hawks and government bankers, would also be carried over and put into place at a later date, and after a different war. Only this time, the economic effects would be far more harmful to US productivity in the long run.

At the close of World War I, the European powers found themselves saddled with colossal debt and embroiled in an era of inflation. The conflict's belligerents had paid for their war expenses in part from debasing their own currencies (some more than others), throwing the gold standard to the side in order to do so. What to do going forward was an immediate concern. Although there was a trickle of underlying impetus to return to gold, it was evident that the enormous amount of currency debasement would clearly prevent a return to gold at the pre-war rate.

Leading the pack on a return to gold was Great Britain, which had enormously debased the pound-sterling during the war. The head of the Bank of England—as well as leading members of parliament—not only wanted to return to gold, but they also insisted that the pound be returned to its 1913 rate of $4.86 (or about 1/4 an ounce of gold). Having entered the war late, the United States escaped the inflation trap and relative to its European counterparts, the dollar emerged in 1918 as the lone prominent currency unscathed by severe debasement. This is significant because the fall-out of the Great War resulted in economic and social chaos throughout the European continent, and though this did not immediately produce direct American military imperialism (the US military quickly demobilized at the close of World War I), it did lead to further "soft-money" attitudes in the United States. The newly established central bank in the United States now had a taste for monetary hegemony.

Different factors paved the way for the international underpinning to the dollar. The economic turmoil and inflation of the pound sealed the fate of London's status as the international financial powerhouse, and in its place would be New York. But as stated, perhaps the most important ingredient to this push for increased US monetary dominance was the newly created Federal Reserve Banking System. Just prior to the war, a long surge of agitation by a consolidated banking lobby finally culminated with the enactment of the Federal Reserve Act, passing through Congress in 1913.

This legislation finally established a central bank for the United States, granting this authority with monopoly-privilege. Competition was ended and replaced with a cartel, led and directed by powerful Big Bankers, all of whom had a vast incentive to continue the lessons they had learned from their monetary experiments during the Spanish-American War. And now, these banking interests had a formal, institutionalized venue to pursue their expansion of monetary hegemony.[30]

The Federal Reserve and the Bank of England devised a scheme to move away from a classical gold standard, and towards a pseudo-gold standard, called the gold-exchange standard. European nations, such as France and Germany, would hold their reserves—or essentially, their savings at their respective central banks—not in gold, but in British pounds. To top this off, the British would hold their reserves in dollars; the only currency still left which was redeemable in gold. This enabled European banks to inflate on top of pounds, and the British could inflate their pounds on top of dollars. This new unstable pyramiding plan—aimed to cure the devastating effects of inflation from the war years—only escalated inflation even further. In fact, the plan was never to actually "cure" inflation, but it was implemented as a means to avoid dealing with the problems the inflation caused, and of course, as is the overall government-banker wish, to permit more inflation in the future.

The gold-exchange standard allowed Britain to evade having to overtly admit their currency debasement, cloaking the new plan in the name of gold, while avoiding the real hard discipline the classical gold standard requires (by 1920, the British pound was likely worth a little over 3 American dollars,

[30] Rothbard, *America's Great Depression*, p.149.

debased from its previous pre-war rate of nearly 5 American dollars). As the international financial leader, Britain found itself in a seemingly impossible situation—insisting on returning to the pre-war rate, all the while knowing this to be impossible with the increased amount of pounds in circulation. The gold-exchange standard was their "solution".

Part of this New York / London agreement was that the Federal Reserve would inflate the dollar as a way to ease this British return to gold at the overvalued rate. Because the gold-exchange standard rested ultimately on the dollar (pounds being the European reserve currency, pounds being exchangeable for their dollar reserves), it was thought that new American inflation could prevent the overvaluation of the British pound from causing an eventual demand by European central banks for dollars, redeemable in gold bullion. And inflate the Fed did. As Murray Rothbard documents in detail in his book *America's Great Depression*, between the years of 1921 and 1929, the new Federal Reserve increased the money supply by over 60%.[31]

Despite this inflation in America, Britain's overvalued pound—detached from gold—acted in the same role as a government-enforced trade barrier. Just as the government tariff artificially raises the prices of imports, Britain's fiat

---

[31] Rothbard, *America's Great Depression*. p.91-95. Also see Phillips, C.A., T.F. McManus, and R.W. Nelson. *Banking and the Business Cycle; A Study of the Great Depression in the United States*. New York: Macmillan, 1937. p.82-84. Phillips, McManus, and Nelson put the 1920s boom into perspective, through the lens of the Austrian theory of the Business Cycle. Their work was largely ignored however, no doubt due to the widespread acclaim given John Maynard Keynes' *General Theory of Employment, Interest, and Money*, published just one year prior.

currency manipulation did the opposite. The overvalued pound raised the prices of Britain's own exports (since all British-made goods are denominated in pounds), and gave the appearance that imports were far cheaper. Between 1920 and 1925 (when the British finally abandoned the gold-exchange standard), the British export industry was severely ravaged. Across the board, export sales were down; some sectors as much as 50%. This British led experiment not only helped fuel the American crash of 1929, but it also provides a telling example of the fatal mistakes the American-led monetary imperialists would saddle the United States with at the close of the next war in the 1940s.

The Roots of the American "Credit Card"

In the wake of World War II, Europe was completely devastated. Six long years of total war and three years of constant Allied bombing left Germany, France, Italy, and the rest of the European heartland in ruins. In was no consequence that American manufacturing boomed in the years to follow, but in reality, many of these US exports were subsidized by our own dollar, giving the boom an artificial lift. Artificial, because after all, if the European market was reduced to rubble, how could the Europeans front the capital to purchase American goods?

The answer was the Marshall Plan, the post-war "stimulus"—which dumped federal grants, subsidies, and American taxpayer loans on the major powers of Europe; its aim to induce economic recovery to the war-torn region. Over the course of six years—between 1945 and 1951, the United States taxpayer poured $25 billion dollars into European industry and economic welfare. This 25 billion is in the context of a total US GDP of $250 billion, or roughly 10% of the United States economy at the time. Stealing money from American manufacturing, redistributing to European industry, and in turn, "giving it back" by "purchasing" American products does not hold up to any sense of economic logic. Individuals who speak against foreign industrial subsidies should be reminded that the Federal Government brought this policy to whole new levels.

But behind these fiscal subsidies lie the central doctrine of this paper—ultimate monetary imperialism. As mentioned already, towards the close of the war, the world's central bankers and financial agents met at Bretton Woods—at the Mount Washington Hotel in a rural area of New Hampshire. This collaboration was aimed at formulating a new international monetary arrangement for the post-war era. Despite representation from John Maynard Keynes, who served as a delegate to the convention as an advisor to the British Treasury, Great Britain was now absent any real, hard influence from its weakened status at war (Keynes' influence on behalf of British national interests was limited, but his influence on economic concepts and the course of the world monetary system was significant). US financial giants—led by the Federal Reserve—achieved unadulterated inflation-power. The pound was out and the dollar was in; going forward, every major sovereign nation would pyramid their currencies on that of the dollar, the new world reserve. After Bretton Woods, theoretically the dollar could still be exchanged for gold bullion by foreign banks and countries—although in practice, the same political pressure would be used against any foreigner which mentioned the word gold. Just as US government bankers had pressured the smaller territories to relinquish their own sound money systems following the Spanish-American War in 1898, so too was the same done after the surrender of the Axis Powers in 1945—only on a much wider scale. US monetary policy had truly succeeded in Dollar Hegemony. The concept had resumed but now with the world as its guinea pig.

The ramifications from the Bretton Woods agreement would take decades to reveal themselves; and at first—the plan created bliss for American bankers and bureaucrats. Economically exhausted, Europeans simply had no capital and so to discuss a dollar-reserve system was moot—for what resources would the French, British, and Germans use to exchange for the dollars to be held in reserve? None, new dollars were printed and "given" to the Europeans. Under the American-financed reconstruction of Europe, the expansion of the dollar poured into the continent. Alongside direct subsidies, the new monetary plan flooded freshly printed US dollars into European banks. For the dollar to act in its new role, more dollars had to be created, surging the inherent tendencies for government and central banks to inflate ever forward.

Of course, the rationale that the new world order needed a "stable" currency at its core was that the dollar-reserve system was still cloaked in the name of gold, the dollar supposedly redeemable at the rate of $35 / per gold ounce (internationally, the dollar had long been off domestic gold redemption). But if what made the dollar stable was gold, then why use the dollar as a reserve? Why not use the source of monetary stability, the classical gold standard? Because the new system was a fraud from the beginning. The dollar's new reserve status permitted the Federal Reserve and their favored banks to inflate ad hoc, as well as accumulate massive amounts of new seigniorage profits and an influx of foreign depositors (in English: More money printing to keep up with the "demand" for new dollars—serving as reserves in foreign banks, along with these new customers in return).

To top this initial government-enforced demand of the dollar, all other currency rates in the world were fixed or "pegged", each one basing their value on American currency. This also meant that all foreign transactions would be denominated in dollars, and with the dollar coercively placed in such "high demand and high supply", there was no immediate limit on the future amount of inflation that could be induced by the Federal Reserve or the US Treasury.

To understand more how this works, pretend a French company would like to purchase goods from Germany. The French would exchange their francs for dollars, pay for the German goods in dollars, and the German producer would then take those dollars and exchange them for marks. This met that, outside of the United States, foreigners were constantly demanding more and more dollars—since the system deliberately forced this "need" for the American induced currency. Of course, many of the dollars that were constantly being printed to supply this "demand", ultimately would have to return to the United States at some point. And here lies another critical part of the perk—the entry point for dollars returning to the US would in large part be major Wall Street clearing houses, all elite members of the Federal Reserve Banking System. The flow of dollars out—and the return of dollars in—the process not derived from the production and consumption of mutually valuable goods, but merely rooted in the production on top of the production of worthless government paper. The Fed produces more dollars, receives more dollars, and lends out more dollars—all while producing nothing of value. The life of the pyramiding scheme continues, not because of real supply and demand of real goods, but merely because the US banking cartel, backed by the full might of an overseas American military presence, says it should.

The "Production" of Dollars for Reserve Use

The production of dollars for foreign use—separate from the function of money merely denominating products of value—has made it ever possible for inflation to flourish. And as mentioned, the effects of inflation from monetary domination causes overarching malinvestments in our domestic economy. Since American markets—especially those first connected to Big Banking—receive these "new" dollars first, American firms command more foreign goods. Over time, the manipulated domestic market has shifted from the sales-starved producer to the consumption driven service-sector. The printed dollars purchase foreign imports—and American retail distributes and consumes the final perishable goods. Restaurants, tourism, hospitality, recreation, retail malls, outlet stores, and supermarkets reign supreme—all revolving around printed American dollars, either injected into circulation directly— or indirectly upon their return from foreign reserves or third party transactions abroad.

But of course, the analysis above would not be complete without including the center of the service-sector industry—the engine that also drives the Welfare and Warfare State—the American banking cartel. As we have already seen, the return dollars perpetuate reduced short-term interest rates, filtering into a glut of credit card bubbles and pyramiding consumption further and further. It should be of no surprise to look at old steel towns like Pittsburgh or Birmingham and see in their stead's—not beacons of manufacturing—but towering skyscrapers of office space, dedicated towards the mass fueling of consumption. Once can simply look at North Carolina, once a productive state ripe with textile and furniture manufacturing; now wiped from the region, replaced with mega Big Banking in Charlotte.

Of course, heaping regulations and direct taxation from both federal and state government has added to the foray; this steady growth of government has wrought its own destruction of commerce—and as pointed out earlier, it is difficult to completely deduce how much of the economic carnage is derived from which source. But it can be deduced with certainty that mammoth bureaucracies and the parasitic Welfare and Warfare State could not come to fruition without the power of the central bank's printing press to finance the growth in the first place. Indeed, the growth of centralized government from Washington has given domestic business little chance of maneuver, no path of escape within the confines of the United States, for if a state government increases its size and power, business can at least relocate. But since the 1970s, the scope of the Federal Government has reached into every part of the American life. Federal bureaucracies now have a "say" over every industry—directly or indirectly. American life in general is politicized.

Education is centralized. Industry has become nationalized. The banks are cartelized. The rate and height of taxation has become ludicrous, and licenses are required for the most mundane economic activity. And just like the malinvestment service sector, the growth of regulations are directly correlated to the growth of bureaucrats, lobbyists, crony capitalists, earmarks, career politicians, trial lawyers, tax accountants, frivolous law suits, and activist judges—activist because the arbitrary laws called regulations grant the power of continued exploitation. All such "investments" represent the wasteful squandering of capital and the misallocation of resources. Due to this increased use of force, the perversion of common law, and the manipulation of freedom, the social benefit conferred by the voluntary accumulation of capital, savings, and hard work is robbed from our civilization. Within this modern context, the driving force of the economy is destroyed. Under this absurd and unsustainable parasite, the market entrepreneur is lost—and even those economic actors who only desire to be left alone must eventually turn to "politics". Violent coercion must be met by force, for this is the only moral justification for which it can be called up.

The fall-out is self-evident. With world-wide reserve currency status, everything denominated in dollars will be numerically higher in price than it otherwise would—when compared to goods or services denominated in a different currency. This is significant—because American exports would be clearly disadvantaged by this artificial trade barrier. Vis-à-vis their international competitors, American produced goods would appear more expensive. This also places the same effect on American goods competing domestically with foreign imports, which overtime appear cheaper to domestic firms. With this coercive implementation of an international dollar standard, a government-induced trade barrier is established. It is not that the dollar is "stronger", for in the beginning of such a process, individuals abroad initiated no demand for the paper dollar in-and-of-itself. However, foreign goods appear to be granted ease of access to American markets. Domestically produced goods though suffer from a non-inclusion of accurate economic calculation—or artificially higher-priced valuations.

In a different light, resources are stealthily stolen from American producers by privileged American bankers—who profit from the creation of more printed dollars and more induced foreign customers forced to use those dollars. In order to profit in this manner, imperialist bankers pull the real capital silently away from the American producer and manufacturer. A free market system? Far from it. Crony-Capitalism? Absolutely. When foreign nations are duped to utilize the dollar, more dollars must be printed. International markets are forced to demand paper dollars from our government, and not valuable goods privately produced from American markets.

The dollars that are continually printed via the ad hoc whims of the Federal Reserve come back through major US banks and have convoluted the meaning of credit. These printed dollars—which formerly served the international role of denominating 2nd and 3rd party foreign exchanges denominated on the "forced-dollar" concept—seep into the domestic

American market in the form of millions and millions of credit cards, or more accurately put, consumption cards. This mega credit binge sold by the American banking industry was ultimately derived from paper printed by the Federal Government. The wave of credit cards plunging into the American market over recent history was not derived from production, but by stealing productive resources and redistributing them through the fractional-reserve "banking" venue. By and large, the majority of this credit is rooted in counterfeit, founded not by the fruits of hard work and voluntary savings, but by the mass-production of government fiat paper.

The Fallacy of the War Boom

Foreign intervention in its most extreme case is war, the initiation of which is not "conservative". Many civilizations which embarked upon such policies—the Greek Empire, the Roman Empire, the British, and the Soviet—all came to a close after the adoption of this financially naïve ideology. Overtime, the war hawks of both major 20th century parties mistook and manipulated the simple policy of defense and replaced it with belligerent offense—aggressive war that this country once despised. Just war can never live on the same plane as aggressive or belligerent combat. The two are diametrically opposed. War of course must only be engaged through the defense of life and property—this is what the history of wisdom tells us. It is indeed necessary at times, but engaging in conflict for reasons that stretch this basic definition will not only lead to careless decisions about the lives of our men and women in uniform, but will eventually help to bankrupt our nation.

Through the continuation of offensive wars around the globe, along with policies such as "nation-building", humanitarian missions based on military occupation, and the deceitful rhetoric of "Making the world safe for Democracy", American foreign policy has leapt from one of humility to empire. With global engagement as the only limit and the projection of “American Exceptionalism” as the national war cry for its justification, Washington continues to call for ever more intervention into the affairs of sovereign nations. For some time now, this has been the political norm, not the exception.

This growth of the American warfare state has worked in the same fashion as any other government agency; much like its domestic counterpart, the welfare state, its framework rests on one large bureaucracy. The major difference is that, while domestic bureaucracy destroys wealth and prosperity, military bureaucracy destroys both wealth and lives. Growing bureaucracy in foreign affairs can lead to "mission creep" or the ever-changing and arbitrary objective of what our foreign policy ends should be, and what means should be applied to achieve these ends. Bureaucracy will always tend to self-perpetuate the expansion of its own existence, and with this expansion, increase power over private property and the market economy. This power of course, also extends to the money supply, perhaps the most vital of all sectors to control.

Before we move on to examine other aspects of recent American foreign policy, let us first realize an unfortunate myth that is still perpetuated in economic circles. The fallacy that somehow, war is “good for the economy”. The reality is, war only destroys—both lives and resources. It does nothing for society on the whole. It can never "boost" the economy, and for those involved survivors, its scars and wounds never leave. However, the economic fallacy that war provides a “stimulus” to economic growth must be debunked. Once this utter lie is seen for what it is, that we can also more-or-less debunk all of Keynesian economics in one fell swoop.

Consider a simple exercise in logic. In order to provide a "war boom", pretend the American nation was put to work building battleships. After the battleships are furnished, they are driven out into the middle of the ocean and blown to smithereens. Now the government buys new ones, and the process is repeated. Sound productive? War boom? The resources to build these battleships are simply squandered on destructive actions. Even if the battleships were not sent to "Davy Jones' Locker", is it economically beneficial to continually build more and more battleships?

Another important dynamic results from these inflation-funded war measures, one that as we have already seen, falls harder on the capital goods sector. The inflation hits the productive structure of the economy by pulling resources to consumer goods production, stripping away capital dedicated to areas more remote from the final end user. Since military expenditures are always oriented for present goods (i.e. consumption), the capital stock is ransacked and a digression of productivity sets in. Considering that the budget for the Department of Defense currently stands at 700 billion dollars (compared to a decade ago, at less than 300 billion), this military spending has also contributed to a huge shift from production to consumption. Combined with inflation, production in capital goods in the United States has long suffered from a continued wartime economy (even in so called "peace"). When overseas spending from the Department of

State, Justice, and other federal bureaucracies are factored in, the total price tag of America's empire is well in excess of one trillion dollars per year.

This new-found direction of land, labor, and capital equipment gives the sudden euphoria of economic health. Joseph Salerno, a well published, astute economist writes:

Under modern conditions, inflationary finance of war involves a government "monetizing" its debt by selling securities, directly or indirectly, to the central bank. The funds thus obtained are then spent on the items necessary to equip and sustain the armed forces of the nation. The result is a sudden expansion of demand for the products of the capital-good industries. A boom is consequently precipitated, featuring rising prices, profits, and stock-values in the former industries. The boom is particularly intense in these industries because, during an inflation, prices rise in temporal sequence. Thus, prices and nominal incomes initially increase only for those sellers who receive the new money in the first round of spending and therefore, before the prices of the productive inputs and consumer goods they themselves regularly purchase have had a chance to rise...War appears to breed universal prosperity.[32]

This myth of the war boom continues today, much in part because of these past economic experiences of euphoric frenzy, but with the same misconceptions that our previous example of

[32] Salerno, Joseph T. "War and the Money Machine: Concealing the Cost of War Beneath the Veil of Inflation". Ch. 19. Denson, John V. *The Costs of War: America's Pyrrhic Victories*. New Brunswick, N.J.: Transaction, 1999. p.449.

Frederic Bastiat's "Broken Window" brings to light—the seen and the unseen. Salerno goes on:

Nonetheless, capital consumption is proceeding apace, with aggregate real losses being suffered especially by higher-order firms. The reason why these firms do not discern their losses and progressive decapitalization is because of their accounting practices, which served them so well during the prewar period of roughly stable prices. Thus, despite the depreciating monetary unit, they continue to carry their fixed capital equipment on their books at historical cost, calculating their depreciation quotas accordingly. Even though some of their costs, especially wage rates, are continually drive up by the inflation-fueled bidding of the producers of military and selected consumer goods, capital-good firms, nevertheless, appear to be earning profits as their output prices continue ever upward with a lag. It is only when it comes to replacing their plant and machinery—possibly years down the road—at the much higher "replacement cost" reflecting monetary depreciation that their decline in capital will at last become evident.[33]

This accounting nightmare runs with the "rotten fish" quandary previously pointed to, but the underlying point is that capital production bears the initial burden of inflation.

But notwithstanding economic logic, this long-standing intellectual blunder of the war boom has also been beefed up

---

[33] Ibid, p. 449-450.

and supported because of a critical episode in 20th century American history. Today, if the history question is asked, "What got us out of the Great Depression?"—many people would likely answer with "World War II". But if, as we have already demonstrated, war can never provide real health to the economy, why does this answer still remain? The start reality is that World War II did not "get us out of the Depression". It did anything but.

As we have covered, the crash of 1929 came as no surprise to the economists from the Austrian School. As Murray Rothbard documented, between the years of 1921 and 1929, the total money supply in the United States had increased by 60%.[34] This expansion of credit—spurred along by the newly created Federal Reserve— bid up the price of capital goods (in this case, much of the newly created credit was allocated towards stocks), much like the most recent crash came after an increase in the supply of money bid up the price of houses and real estate. When the inevitable bust came, prices on the stock market crashed, all at once, wiping out the phony wealth that was created from the preceding boom period.

Under President Herbert Hoover's lesser known interventionary schemes, and then later Franklin Roosevelt's more notorious New Deal policies, make-work programs and banking holidays came to the forefront of American policy. This new domestic doctrine, conceptually resembling the George W. Bush / Barack Obama bail-out and stimulus programs, served to transition the initial downslide of recession

---

[34] Rothbard, *America's Great Depression*, p.91-95.

into the prolonged economic era known as the Great Depression. This vast domestic intervention aggravated the necessary market corrections—resources were continually misallocated, the labor force was prevented from returning to private enterprises demanded by the consumer, and high unemployment numbers were kept alive via the government's refusal to allow the liquidation of malinvestment and unsustainable debt from the credit induced "Roaring 20s".

But these massive government expenditures paled in comparison to the government spending brought on by World War II. However, 1941—and the wartime years that followed—did not bring economic prosperity. To the contrary, central bureaucratic planning, government rationing, and price controls in support of the war effort forced residents on the home front to go without. In essence, resources that would have otherwise went to producing goods and services for the consumer were diverted to goods and services for the government's war production. Consumers were forced to abstain from present consumption, in order to "free up" resources for the war. Instead of building cheaper, more affordable cars, Detroit was requisitioned to build more and more tanks. Yet some would say that the unemployment phenomenon was "cured"; looking more closely though, if millions and millions of American citizens are drafted into foxholes in Europe, unemployment is indeed "solved".

It is simple to understand why people are still misled into believing the fallacy of the war boom. After all, it is easy to *see* all the workers under one roof making bombs and tanks. But we must also come to realize that which is goes *unseen*—all of the resources the central government confiscates from producers spread throughout the markets of the country, in order to subsidize the concentrated workers within the various *seen* weapons factories.

True to form, these same Keynesian intellectuals—who had claimed World War II "alleviated" the Depression and who by 1946 had overtaken the economics profession—screamed to the high heavens that the country would face another economic depression once the war was ended. Millions of men would be returning from military service in Europe and the Pacific, and the Keynesians, who illogically hold to the belief that a shortage of consumption and spending are behind economic depressions, ignominiously warned of an impending economic catastrophe if colossal stimulus programs were not placed into action to accompany the military demobilization. Fortunately this advice was ignored; and ultimately, what the Federal Government did do was to cut the central budget by over 60%, while taxes were reduced by a substantial margin. These spending cuts relinquished vital resources to the market economy, finally permitting American markets—starved for capital for nearly 15 years— to respond. The ensuing result was not depression, but one of the greatest periods of economic growth in US history. In essence, the Great Depression ended, not from World War II, but post-World War II—when government finally became smaller again. What truly provides economic prosperity is not war, but peace.

War is the Health of the State

The results from Big Government policies to "solve a problem" in foreign matters are not in the least bit different conceptually from domestic ones. Blowback, or unintended consequences from foreign intervention, is often the result of American military action abroad. Unlike domestic intervention, unintended consequences from foreign intervention are more difficult for the American public at large to place into context, as many times US policy makers have acted beforehand in a non-transparent manner.

Nonetheless, blowback works very much the same way as domestic regulation into the otherwise free economy, for at its root, blowback is the unforeseen results of American meddling in to foreign internal matters. However, because of their foreign nature and the collision of different cultures and societies in non-market methods (i.e. violence), these unintentional effects can be much more dramatic or severe.

Over the past few decades, hatred for the United States has been mounting throughout the different corners of the world. But the cause of this resentment and hatred does not rest from some unknown, mystical reason. Still to this day, many politicians stand up and tell us that "We are just so free. The rest of the world hates our freedom." How ludicrous! This foreign resentment comes about because we have been sticking our nose in someone else's business! 200 years ago, our ancestors revolted against a foreign power for merely taxing the tea they drank and the stamps they used. How can it not be understood, that More invasion and more war initiation will only further weaken our Republic and spread our forces thin—and foreign hatred will often manifest itself into determined armed attack, sometimes in the form of terrorism, as it so often has in the recent past. These policies of nation-state building and policing the world are doomed to failure, an inevitable result that has wasted American and foreign lives in the process, along with trillions in wealth. Initiating foreign conflict—especially without a Constitutional Declaration—leads to endless war. But it causes other detrimental and undesirable results as well.

Once the entity of central government is granted more power—the sphere of its influence can never be managed or constricted into one sector of life over the other. It must always tend to spread, and inevitably corrode the fabric of civil and economic liberties of its domestic citizens. If the power is granted to centralized government in one area, then it is by default implicitly granted the power to do it in another. Once centralized government gains enough power to invade a foreign nation, the way in which this power is used can no longer be kept contained. The true check of power is private property, and once the right of private property to ownership and use becomes less recognizable by government, the extent of government coercion becomes less contained. It becomes easier to compel the general citizenry into the purchase of health care insurance, or the authority to tax carbon dioxide is endowed by bureaucrats. This is a lesson from the Hayekian Road to

Serfdom.[35]However, the trend of conflict continues, and our country's overseas conflicts have escalated. Most disturbing is that ever since this pattern began, whereby our country unconstitutionally goes to war without a proper Declaration from the Congress (as mandated by Article I Section 8)—our nation's government has practically been engaged in one long continual state of war for over 60 years—and this is seen today as nothing unusual!

Conflict begets conflict, and so long as an American military presence remains spread throughout the "frontier", there will always be new monsters to slay. In fact, when American history is examined, we can also derive that government provides this wide-spread acceptance by the public that all of these endless wars are "good" and "just". Much of this propaganda has been rooted in fear and emotion, and certainly not logic. These past wars have been sold to the public with warnings about the need to stop the world's next Hitler. The sales pitch runs something like this, "Well, there's a boogey man out there, and you have to give us the power to stop him. Don't believe us? Well, just take my word for it." The latest boogey man has become the "Islamic Fascist", the "Terrorist", or the Iranian "Radical".

And so a major question persists—when did the public accept this supposedly "conservative" position, which has now

---

[35] Hayek, Friedrich A. Von. *The Road to Serfdom: Text and Documents*. Ed. Bruce Caldwell. Vol. II. Chicago: University of Chicago, 2007. In Hayek's classic work written at the close of WWII, an underlying theme throughout is that centralized power cannot be restricted or confined to one sphere of individual life over another. Once ower is ceded over economic life, than power will likely encroach on civil life (and vice-versa).

become the endorsement of foreign offensive war and fear mongering? If you look back in history, taking the nation to entangling wars used to stand as the radical, unaccepted position! Although the ideas of foreign intervention and Empire had already begun to foment, Woodrow Wilson became the champion and intellectual author of the tag line mentioned earlier: "Make the World Safe for Democracy". Woodrow Wilson—even more so than Theodore Roosevelt—was one of the more significant leaders of the "Progressive Era"—a radical shift in American history that helped place the final nails in the coffin of a decentralized American Republic. Wilson's foreign policy ideas of increased intervention coincided directly with massive domestic intervention into the market economy. Woodrow Wilson presided over the establishment of the Federal Income Tax and the Federal Reserve Banking System, centralizing power in Washington—permitting bureaucratic authorities to directly confiscate personal income, and giving the power to the Federal Government to debase, and counterfeit currency. Wilson also championed the change in how US Senators were chosen, shifting the process from one of appointment by the various state legislatures, to a direct popular vote from the public at large—ending one of the last true checks the individual state governments had over Federal power and mob rule. Simultaneously, the Wilson Administration played national nanny, banning alcohol across the entire continent, after its use was deemed by bureaucrats as "immoral for the public" (giving rise to the organized cartels of the Prohibition Age). It's safe to say, these ideas were not shared by the early Founders.

This domestic intervention, and the erosion of private property rights, gave Wilson and others like him only increased and ever-heightened power. The Wilson Administration went on to ignore the advice of our country's Founders—who eerily warned of the entangling political alliances of Europe—and by 1917, the United States fell into the blood-soaked trenches of Europe. Over the course of just one year, 100,000 Americans had lost their lives during World War I. And for what? If we look back on the prevailing thoughts of this point-in-time, the counter opinion, the "conservative opinion", was to stay out of the war. Discretion, restraint, and wisdom, all ignored in favor of power. As was pointed out, war is bad for the economy, and contrary to popular opinion now, many at this time knew that war was bad for business—for currency devaluation (bringing about the initial concealed prosperity) was still in its infancy. What's more is that the entrance of the United States onto the battlefields of Europe ended the teetering back-and-forth stalemate, and provided a one-way victory for the British Empire: Winner take-all, and Loser pay-all.

It's important to note that in this day-of-age, it was never a foregone conclusion that the United States would ever "side" with the British—or the French, in any war. In fact, many Americans had just as much in common with the Germans. By the end of the 19th century, a huge influx of immigrants from Germany and Eastern Europe had poured into the United States. In addition, a significant portion of the American population was now of direct Irish descent—who looked upon the English Parliament as despotic tyrants. And up until this time, the United States was still very wary about the British Empire—just as Germany was (after all, we had already fought two wars against it). It is very likely, that in the absence of American intervention, the European powers would have had to deal with a cease-fire and the end of hostilities in their own way. Resources and lives had depleted on both sides so severely, that neither was in a position to dictate any terms of surrender, and certainly not an unconditional one. But this was not to be.

The "Woodrow Wilson-plunge" pushed one side clearly over the top—but needless to say, all of the European powers lay in utter bankruptcy after the war. Out of hatred and frustration, the Allies, especially the French, forced inconceivable war reparations onto the Germans—who were now the most bankrupt of all. The war reparations, punishing German payments to the victorious Allies, were conceptually impossible for the Germans to pay from the get-go. In fact, a mere five years after these impossible payments were forced upon Germany—by none other than the full weight and force of American intervention—hyperinflation began to run its course through the German economy, as the German government had tried turning to the printing-press to finance its deficits, and social programs. By December of 1923, the German paper currency had become utterly worthless. Piles of German Marks lined the streets and sidewalks of Berlin, simply discarded as garbage, its purchasing power completely depleted. Complex exchange came to a grinding halt, and much of the

German population was forced into localized barter just to eat. Inflation had ruined what was left of German commerce and trade—more so than the actual hardships from the war—and years of suffering lingered on. In from the chaos and the starvation rolled the beginnings of the Third Reich. Blaming the Jews and the bankers for all German miseries, the Nazi Party won the elections of 1930. Power had increased in Germany, it had not diminished. In other words, another boogey man was found.

But oh, how history has been perverted! This interpretation of events is not found in public school books today. Universities still lecture about America's excursion into the blood-filled trenches as its first step towards assuming its rightful place in the world, a polluted neo-version of Manifest Destiny. To the contrary, greater American leadership was forfeited by a very real result of sacrificing American sovereignty and independence at the altar of the soon-to-be United Nations. Those who dissent from these flawed policies of today are quickly scorned as "unpatriotic"—or perhaps naive "isolationists". But what truly isolates our country is the continual military intervention throughout the globe. Trade and commerce never isolates, but sticking our nose in someone else's business does. Our very financial well-being depends on how quickly we can relearn this lesson.

The initiation of war cannot long endure on the same plane with a free society. One policy must first fall, freedom or war mongering. Notwithstanding, belligerent war—the ultimate negation of the American tradition—has become the status-quo for our nation. And belligerent war has a tendency to spread. Both political parties, even the so-called "small government" party, have slowly corrupted themselves with the policies of war hawks and defense lobbyists. This has not happened overnight, but it has most certainly happened. One cannot defend freedom by destroying private property. The two are always linked.

Growth of the Warfare State under Inflation

The growth of the American warfare state did not begin with the Wilson Administration, but certainly, the 28th head-of-state did anything but curb it (we have already pointed to the precedent set by Abraham Lincoln). Moral and constitutional grounds begot, more fitting to the premise of this work rests a more significant element of the Statist warfare trend. Given the context that such a policy, adopted for so long a period, costs nothing short of a fortune to the public at large, how does such a policy of foreign intervention continue? Only an inflationary monetary policy—controlled by centralized government—can support this appetite for military adventurism. Inflation is the optimal tool to finance such endeavors, as the crushing price to the market producer is hidden. In fact, this mechanism has been the method of choice for centralized governments, old and new. Typically, one can determine a correlation between the size and scope of centralized government and the "honesty" of its money.

For instance, the Roman coin, the denarius, was more or less the predominant currency of its time throughout the western world—reaching past the frontiers of the Roman Empire. At 100% silver, the denarius stood for centuries as a reliable medium of exchange. As the Roman Empire expanded, a long successive line of emperors began to slowly erode the silver content of this sound currency to finance the growing needs of the Roman treasury. By the 3rd Century, the denarius was debased so severely, that hardly a fraction of the coin contained silver. The coins were continually diluted with "cheap" metals, and by the 4th Century, the denarius was merely dipped with a coated silver glaze.[36] Inflation ran wild in Rome proper, and the military forces the Emperors had built up demanded ever more payment. Toward the latter days of the Roman Empire, all sorts of gimmicks were tried to continue Roman military power abroad. Of significant note, the "Barbarian" troops by this time, who were mercenaries hired en-mass as supplements to the Legions, demanded payment only in gold. By the end of the 5th Century A.D. the Roman Empire in the West had collapsed in financial ruin.

Of particular historical significance and one that is less commonly studied, is the Spanish Empire—which shared a

---

[36] Peden, Joseph. *"Inflation and the Fall of the Roman Empire"*, LewRockwell.com. 18 Aug. 2009. Web. <http://www.lewrockwell.com/orig10/peden1.1.1.html>. Peden gives brief remarks on Edward Gibbon's classic work, *The Fall and Decline of the Roman Empire*, first published in 1776, in which he states that even Gibbon's huge historiography often failed to conclude how the Roman civilization lasted as long as it did, given the scope of the Roman government's consumption. Peden states that inflation enabled the Roman Authority to pursue policies that led to its demise. But he writes that inflation can never be understood apart from the centralized government. As he states, "My analysis is based on the premise that monetary policy cannot be studied, or understood, in isolation from the overall policies of the state. Monetary, fiscal, military, political and economic issues are all very much intertwined. And the reason they are all so intertwined is, in part, due to the fact that the state, any state, normally seeks to monopolize the supply of money within its own territory."

similar experience as the late Roman one. By the early 16th Century, Spain had become the predominant military power on the European continent. Under the House of Habsburg, Charles V built up the warfare state of the Spanish regime—and was first to realize the major military reach to the Americas—and the subsequent expropriation of this resource rich New World. Large quantities of gold and silver were seized from the South and Central Americas, loaded on Spanish ships to be imported back to the European continent. But military conquest was by far limited to the natives of America. Spanish military campaigns against France, the Ottoman Empire, and the German "Protestant" provinces all took their toll—and foreign lenders, even with pledged collateral from newfound treasures from the Incas and Aztecs—refused their capital altogether. Ironically, this huge influx in stolen precious metals from the New World greatly accelerated inflation, increasing the money supply within the Spanish empire. However, confounding this growing inflationary problem was the Spanish regime's monetary policy of debasing its own currency. During this era, one of the most notorious offenders of currency devaluation was Charles V himself. A fabulous "counterfeiter", in 1537 Charles V ordered the public treasury to devalue his Empire's currency, shifting the gold-to-silver ratio from 10.1 to 1 to 10.6 to 1.[37] But by this time, Charles has already implemented several machinations of currency tricks, always aimed at "lightening" the real debt burden that his policies continually

---

[37] Erlichman, Howard J. *Conquest, Tribute, and Trade: The Quest for Precious Metals and the Birth of Globalization*. Amherst, NY: Prometheus, 2010. p.200.

placed on his regime. This devaluation is similar of course to modern Federal Reserve policy of "quantitative easing".

This was to no avail, for the consuming appetite of government was pushing private production under. Several times the Spanish government was forced to declare bankruptcy, and renegotiate loans at unfavorably high interest rates. By the late 1570s, Spain's military expenditures—in no small part financed by inflation—were greater than all of the other major European Powers combined. Spain continued its warfare spending, and in spite of their dwindling resources, the Spanish regime persisted with its policy of "military glory", even after several government defaults during this period. After a long string of lavish military campaigns in France, the Algiers, and Germany, Charles V's regime teetered on bankruptcy. When interest from foreign loans became too burdensome (some of which neared 50% interest rates), the debasement of the Spanish currency, and Spanish "securities", only increased. But by this time, many of Charles' creditors demanded real treasure from the Americas, nothing less.[38] By the late 1500s, the Spanish regime—in spite of all its loot from the New World—had consumed vast amounts of wealth. Charles V's government underwent several formal defaults, and by the close of the 16th century, the Spanish Empire had come to a ruinous financial end.

The historical example of Charles V provides an excellent context for which to see the fruits of military expansion. Yet it is only with government counterfeiting that such a policy can

---

[38] Ibid, p.229-230.

be exaggerated for any given time period. The market must produce wealth—and as this wealth is produced via complex exchange—it can be more readily seized by confiscated not the wealth itself, but the medium through which it is transferred.

Part V

The Centralization of Power

Marx and Keynes: Control of the Money Supply

As the world entered the industrial revolution some 150 years ago, a publication was released in the west advocating the end of private property. It was claimed that only then could real freedom be achieved. Karl Marx's *Communist Manifesto* outlined his thoughts on how to achieve these ends—and though Marx believed his magnum opus to be something of an original work, in reality, this idea of institutionalized force is as old as the human race.

Marx ignored the natural order of property, insisting that though the measures to achieve these end objectives may be brutal at first, the ends would justify the means. His belief that the market entrepreneur's profits were simply a "surplus charge", and that once this was forced down, or essentially eliminated, labor would achieve a higher standard of living. Briefly examining this claim of "surplus charging", which can still be heard today as "price-gouging", we can determine the crux of the argument is erroneous. Profits on the market are the prices paid for change. Thought markets tend towards equilibrium, they will never reach such a static state. In a totally "at rest" economy, with no change, no shift in time preference or choice, there would be no profit. But since human beings are constantly changing throughout the course of life, market decisions must change as well. Under the free economy, the rate of profit then is determined by this rate of change. As the consumers continually change their commands, profits are paid for the amount of work done to constantly shift supply and demand to their new levels. However, as we have discussed, change through this process in the free economy is done through peaceful and well-coordinated methods. Marx's analysis ignores that someone must perform the work to change, someone must "step up to the plate". As we have discussed, that "someone" is the market entrepreneur. The natural rate of profit then depends on the size and scope of the change at hand—the job "asked" of the market entrepreneur.

A large part of Marx's argument is cluttered with emotionally-charged criticism. He authored his work at a time of great economic and social change, and his charges to the capitalist system were based primarily on those things seen by the naked eye. For instance, this can be seen in Marx's economic treatise, *Capital*, which was first published in 1867 (though after his death in 1883, more volumes would be released by his German socialist partner Freidrich Engels). During this time period, the Industrial Revolution was well underway. Factories of mass production had been constructed, employing thousands of new workers from different walks of life. By modern standards, many of these factories had relatively poor working conditions, and could be dangerous environments indeed. Marx's thought process looked at these "evils" and concluded this to be slavery. However, what Marx did not do was look at conditions prior to the factor. It is easy to see all the new workers, concentrated under one roof, and claim inhumane treatment. But it is more difficult to see where these workers came from previous to the investment of capital in plant equipment and factories. Dispersed throughout the countryside, under many different roofs, their standard of living was far worse. Food was more scarce, shelter more expensive. The very fact that workers chose new employment, that is, that they opted to accept the new offers at the factory is substantially significant in rationale deduction. For to pull workers from former roles of employment to new ones, better conditions must be offered, not worse. Most of the time, these "better conditions" are reflected in a wage premium, or higher income. Despite all the horror stories about early factories, little light is ever shed on the real horrors of starvation and back-breaking work by hand that existed before these factories were born from real savings.

Marxism is merely a distant forerunner to its later cousin, Keynesianism. Keynes also denied natural law under private property, but moreover, believed that market "failure" belonged to interest rates; that if lowered, prosperity would surely follow. Marx held this same belief, only placing his focus on profits as a whole. To Keynes, the banker who charged interest for his service, he was the demon. Interest was the price that had to go. To Marx, all businessmen were holding back the advancement of society. Under the Marxian view, all profits—which together help determine the much greater market rate of interest—were holding back the progress of civilization. Though Marx believed his methods would become reality through *revolution*—or that these aforementioned "evils" would be righted through an overnight change in the status-quo—what has actually transpired throughout the western world's democracies was the slow *evolution* of more and more power vested in the hands of the State. The past century has not been an age of "unbridled" capitalism—but rather one of unfettered State-intervention and planning.

It is important to realize that the names of these interventionist institutions are irrelevant. Communism, Socialism, Fascism, or what we embrace today—Democratic Progressivism—it matters not what form the intervention takes. The economic outcome is more or less the same in either variety of government-controlled schemes—for the effect is undisturbed by the selection method chosen. This analysis has eluded many historians and economists. The Soviet Union did not fail because of socialism under a "dictatorship", for socialism under a "democracy" produces the same economic result. It is not the particulars of the government selection process which causes economic destruction. The failure comes from crossing such a precipice—that plans should not be made by the individual but by bureaucracy. The underlying detriment to prosperity comes from permitting any government entity the assumption of this economic power in the first place.

A large intellectual failure stems from how these two flawed economic theories have achieved widespread "credibility". It was the business cycle, caused by the expansion of bank credit, orchestrated en-masse by central banking, which fomented the social chaos. Accordingly, this social disarray allowed the seeds for such radically illogical ideas to grow. These ideas, from either Marx or Keynes, are only given legitimacy precisely because of the social confusion from the business cycle. Ideas shape the course of history, and their ideas would fail to be taken seriously without the social upheaval from government-created depression.

In 1931, a short time after the Wall Street crash in New York—Keynes was being held up as an intellectual giant in London. The British Parliament asked him to preside over a government hearing aimed at addressing the British economy, which was entering depression itself. The committee was entertaining some of his most recent ideas, published in his 1930 book, *A Treatise on Money.*[39] Within this work, Keynes asserted his so-called "Paradox of Savings"; that if people saved too much, others would be thrown out of work, and depression would surely result (of course, as we have already discussed, when individuals abstain from present consumption, they merely free up resources for others to increase capital production—ensuring that the savers will have more goods in the future to purchase). Keynes literally went on the airwaves in London, telling housewives to go out and spend their savings, and continue to shop. For this was their patriotic duty, to boost employment by spending and spending. In the midst of depression, who knows how many were ruined by such advice. Regardless, power needs flawed intellect to justify itself, and

---

[39] Keynes, John Maynard. *A Treatise on Money.* New York: Harcourt, Brace and Company, 1930.

government policy in Britain—and the United States—began to embrace such lunacy. (Interesting enough, even some of his contemporaries in the economics field within Britain considered Keynes to be a "quack").[40]

Also important to understanding the pivotal role inflation played with these central planners was the emphasis upon which both Marx and Keynes placed on State-control over the money supply. In Keynes' *Treatise On Money*, his idea for a world-wide central bank, and common international fiat currency was established.

Turning to Marx, underneath his systematic plan for social utopia was, indeed, a call for control of the money supply. In his "10 Pillars of Communism" was a blueprint for the necessary steps the State need follow before a fully-socialized system could come to be. Interesting enough was Marx's 5th pillar, and the adoption by nearly every "sophisticated" western government since:

> **5. Centralization of credit in the hands of the State, by means of a national bank with State capital as an exclusive monopoly.**[41]

Perhaps this is the most intriguing point of Marxism, the establishment of the central bank. There is no greater means for

---

[40] Wapshott, Nicholas. *Keynes Hayek: The Clash That Defined Modern Economics*. New York: W.W. Norton & Company, 2011. p.64.

[41] Marx, Karl, and Friedrich Engels. *The Communist Manifesto and Other Writings*. Comp. Martin Puchner. New York: Barnes & Noble, 2005. p.28.

the State to escalate its power than through the monopoly of the mint…and no greater means to discombobulate market exchange, while simultaneously blaming free enterprise as the cause. Our country's unfortunate path towards this 5th "pillar" was completed in 1913, with the establishment of the Federal Reserve banking cartel. Since this period—with this vast monetary means at its disposal, the central government has printed its way towards the acquisition of increased resources.

But contrary to Marx's entire rationale, this process does not favor the "worker" or the lower class, but quite the opposite. The State inflates its way towards more power—and in doing so, robs from the poor by eating away at their savings, as increased prices on goods and services are at first, felt hardest by the poor. Prices go up and real wages continue downward, as money wages on the whole are typically the last price to go up during the transition from a smaller money supply to a larger one. This is the more explicit and telling tenant for Statist ideas. Marx's outline does not point to democratic rule by the "lower class" but rather rule in itself. How better to increase government's reach than to slowly expand the size of such power by hiding its immediate costs through the slow march of inflation? Direct taxation can cause social unrest, but it can be years before the full effect of, say, our Federal Reserve's money printing schemes surface to the public. By this time, the State has reached epic levels of power and bureaucracy, and can be well-prepared to enforce draconian rules to crush resistance.

Even then, the results are simply blamed on the very thing the Statist desires to eliminate: the free market. The chaos at the hands of the monopoly central bank "frames" the market for the booms and busts we constantly bear witness to in today's modern economy. Through price-fixing and artificial interest rates, the Federal Reserve has created boom after boom and all the malinvestment which runs with this sickness is perturbed further by disallowing market correction. Recessions—the key to healing the malinvestment—are prolonged by continued money printing, all the while damaging the integrity of our nation's currency. Manufacturing, in favor of present consumption, has dissipated, and the symptoms of heightened government corruption, economic depression, and price inflation are products of this tenant.

Social Turmoil

As of yet, we have only examined the economic consequences from this growing inflation. But there are serious social concerns that are become evident as well. To understand the social turmoil that will eventually come about, we must look at how this inflation has shaped the livelihoods of US citizens.

Naturally, these economic effects spill over into social life. We have briefly mentioned several in the aggregate. Inflation has distorted the US economy, leaving wide swaths of the population with higher prices for necessities. It has altered the family unit by forcing both parents to work, and both are now far more likely to do so through employment in the service sector. However, this is only the tip of the iceberg and does not spell out the multitude of economic and social consequences at play for the coming age. These inflationary forces have also worked in simultaneous fashion to change the choices, the behavior, the experience, and hence, the social future for a new generation of Americans.

Unfortunately, the financing of centralized government through inflation has proven to be an extremely effective one. This growth has led to enormous subsidies in higher education, as previously pointed to, large expenditures on the military. The untold social damage from this government intervention is hard to measure, but it can be deduced. As the youth of America mature, the replacement of private production with government bureaucracy forces old choices to become nonexistent, while creating conditions that lead many down the path of permanent injury. To see this in at work, let's begin by looking at an adolescent who is now faced with life decisions. Upon graduating from high school, the forces of bureaucracy shape these choices, either through various incentives, or by restricting the opportunities that would have been available.

Many high school students are presented with few real job opportunities. As government has soaked up more and more capital, what remains has been the choices left in this wake. With broad direction from the government planners, many face college or the military. Government subsidies, mainly in the form of Federal loans, provide high school students with a strong incentive to go on to college. True to form, more college degrees are awarded today more than ever. This does not however mean the nation is more educated. Nor does it mean university diplomas equate to higher income. Part of the "welfare state" fabric is tied to the rhetoric of education. Education for all, and for those deemed less privileged or less fortunate, equal opportunity. In reality, the state's attempt to provide equal opportunity has provided equal share in debt. Before they have ever earned a dime, many college students today graduate thousands of dollars in debt.

However it is often argued, now more individuals are educated. They can earn more income, and the debt is justified. This is backwards analysis. The bureaucrat claims an engineer earns more money on the market. He learned engineering in college. Hence, if more people only had engineering degrees, more people would enjoy higher salaries. Only the market first demanded someone with the skills and talents of the engineer. The fact that the engineer was taught these skills in college is more or less besides the point. At any one time, there are only so many jobs on the market which require the skills of an engineer. This fact does not change when Federal subsidies augment the number of individuals pursuing engineering degrees. All other factors aside, this could actually lead to lower salaries for all engineers, at the expense of existing ones already on the market. As new engineers loaded with government loans saturate the work force, the newer subsidized engineers will tend to accept salaries below the existing market rate. The heavy burden of debt these subsidized engineers carry only stands to further increase this downward force on income. Afforded with this opportunity to pay less in wages to engineers, private firms that demand engineering work would benefit at the expense of existing "pre-subsidy" engineers, and ultimately at the expense of the tax payer.

In addition to this quantitative dilemma, perhaps a much more troubling problem is the quality of education. There are only so many individuals capable of comprehending complex concepts. Most individuals lack the faculty for advanced physics, or medicine. Despite all external factors, nothing can change the absence of innate ability. Scores of university professors cannot lift these natural limitations. Einstein's theories can never be mastered if this intrinsic aptitude is lacking. Only some have the entrepreneurial foresight to become captains of industry, or the physical prowess to become kings on the baseball diamond. Accordingly, very few can be Einstein.

As the Federal subsidies artificially increase the demand for higher education, college enrollment goes up. But higher enrollment on campus does not lift the limitations of these new students' capabilities. Because of this dilemma, the quality of education—or what is being taught—begins to suffer. The curriculum is debased. Instead of standards aimed ever upwards, downward pressure is placed on the campus syllabus. Teaching shifts towards the lowest common denominator. For instance, to graduate more engineers, less engineering must be taught (or the standards are lowered). Some departments begin to teach "quack" ideas and the field of economics has been debased as such. But this effect of academic deprivation is not limited to department. Typically, new curricula are "invented". Since the increased supply of college students has translated into an increased level of limitation per student (or less overall capability for the student population on the whole), an overabundance of degrees in liberal arts, management, or "fuzzy" majors are offered. Universities spend less time and effort on the professions of the market, and more time and effort on subjects less demanded by the private sector. By and large, markets have very little use for individuals who spend years studying basket weaving. The connection between market demand and college supply is shattered.

The subsidies do however alter the broader economy as well, first and foremost by removing large portions of the labor force from the market. Over time, this creates shortages for existing businesses, which begin to find it increasingly difficult to replace their retiring or aging workforce with reliable personnel. Under natural conditions, a student intent on continuing their education must pay their own way, from real, existing savings. True, these savings can come from the student's own work, their parents, a private loan or scholarship. But in all cases, the prospective student or family must value college education more than the amount of savings that such a diploma would consume. In other words, potential students are left to judge whether the benefits of higher education exceed the level of savings required to attend. Longer term thinking is, again, encouraged and fostered. Students tend to look towards the future post-college environment, to determine whether the investment is worth their private savings. Savings from parents or private scholarship sources act in the same manner. If the investment is not valued high enough, their savings are withheld and used elsewhere. This method of finance—rooted in private savings—not only ensures that colleges compete on academic value, ever increasing the scholastic quality offered, but it also causes prices to fall, not rise. But under the Federal subsidies, this trend of longer term thinking is strongly discouraged. A general lowering of individual time preferences takes place. In greater numbers, college students who entered campus intent on studying more difficult courses—courses which yield greater dividends in the future—may now opt to take an easier path in the present, simply because this easier path exists in bigger supply. In order to enjoy the "party scene" of leisure with friends, more students tend to choose one of the aforementioned "invented" fields that now exists as an alternative, yet one which will carry very little return in their older years.

This next point brings us to the cost of higher education, which over recent years has exploded throughout the country. The flare-up of price is easy to see with the naked eye, and is far above the massaged "inflation rate" calculated by the central government. For instance, the tuition at the University of California Berkley was $700 a year in the 1970s. Today it is over $15,000 a year—a 2,000% increase. Even tuition rates at more traditional schools, such as West Virginia University, have skyrocketed. In little over a decade, tuition rates have more than doubled at WVU. Even for in-state students who receive a price-break, the tuition at West Virginia University has jumped from $2,700 in the year 2000 to over $5,600 a year today. This price is no longer a function of student and campus, but a function of Federal inflation. Because of the nature of subsidies, college universities have long ceased competing against one another on price, but instead compete on the attraction of Federal subsidies. Price becomes less consequential when students no longer make decisions about "if" they should carry on their education, but only "where" they should carry on their education. Because of the ease of choosing college (with the price covered for the immediate future), colleges and universities have ignored cost reduction and savings, in order to keep prices down. Instead, lavish spending on recreational facilities and athletic departments are aimed at drawing the student to spend "their" Federal dollars at these larger, more luxurious campuses. All in all, more present thinking is fostered at the expense of the long term—from the perspective of the student and from the point of the university staff.

However, it is truly the mechanism by which these Federal subsidies take shape that has the gravest effect on the cost of higher education. Much of these higher education subsidies come about as federally guaranteed bank loans. These loans are granted to any prospective student meeting very minimal criteria. With the Federal Government's "guarantee", participating banks realize no risk and short-run thinking is encouraged—between both parties to the exchange. On the one hand, the student, who merely looks to college without the immediate consideration of burdensome costs; and, on the other, the bank, which looks upon such a loan as an "asset", one which can never be discharged from this student's liability, even through bankruptcy. This point is often telling—by federal mandate, this future debt is prioritized ahead of all creditors, even to escape the venue of Constitutional Bankruptcy Court—for it is the banker's interests which have often driven these federal programs, not the student's. And so as more bank loans are placed into universities and colleges across the country, the tuition price is bid up.

Under natural circumstances, absent this government intervention, the price would indeed tend to fall—for if colleges depended on personal savings—either from the individual, the individual's parents, or private scholarships—then prices must be justified. The colleges bid for business, and bidding pressure is ever downward. But we can see, with government, the reverse holds true.

With this price inflation, there is one more major remaining factor, as of yet unanalyzed. Through the fractional-reserve banking process, the money pumped into tuition is created from nothing. Pell Grants and direct tax dollars only fund a small minority of federal subsidies. The vast majority of the mega spending on college comes from large banks participating in federal programs, or outright government enterprises, such as Sallie Mae and others, which have either implicit government guarantees or special privileges, allowing them to attract more capital to their firms than what they otherwise could. From this point, the fractional-reserve process begins. Much of the federally backed loans spilling forth from these major lenders are expanding credit off of a tiny amount of reserve deposits in their vaults, creating a great pyramiding effect. From this huge numeric total of dollars going to college loans, only a small ratio represents real prior savings. Real savings have once again, become diluted in mountains of "counterfeit". Thus, not only are resources being misdirected from the Federal guarantee, going to campuses when they otherwise would be going elsewhere, but the credit expansion—unbacked by real savings—pushes the numeric prices of tuition to levels far above what even the typical government tax subsidy could achieve. If college subsidies were merely tax dollars redistributed to prospective students, the price would still reflect real resources (only redirected from their original owners).

The higher prices seen today are not simply tax dollars redistributed by the central government. They are a reflection of a vast credit expansion from the increase of the money supply centrally directed into university tuition. This difference may seem semantic, but the students accepting these loans are left with astronomical debt after graduation (if they graduate at all)., This debt is numerically higher than what it would otherwise be, even if students financed tuition through subsidies stemming from direct tax dollars. True to form, over one trillion dollars worth of college debt is now outstanding. An entire generation of Americans have indeed attended "higher education"—and next to a lifetime of debt and a hollow degree—have little to show for it.

For a young man or woman coming of age, another major force has played on their life decisions and opportunities. Every year, the mammoth military expenditures of the national government enroll hundreds of thousands of American adolescents into the country's armed forces. The overt "defense" spending of the United States has more than doubled in a decade, from less than $300 billion in the year 2000, to more than $700 billion today. It is by far the largest military budget in the world. Gone are the days that the United States "demobilized" in the wake of war. Today, the United States finds virtually unlimited "enemies" from which to secure the nation's supposed interests. Taken with other forms of government spending overseas, such as the State Department and other such bureaucracies involved, the American Empire easily consumes over one trillion dollars from the economic productivity of the market. But as immense as this figure seems, this flagrant government spending devours more than just this numeric tally of dollars given. It substantially alters the future of millions of Americans by squeezing out productive market opportunities. As this crowding out effect escalates, young Americans find fewer jobs left in the market. For those that do not succumb to the lure of subsidized college, the military can present a financially rewarding alternative. With the many benefits promised after such service, including those perks involving paid higher education, the leviathan state of spending again draws much of the population into its central plans.

With more young Americans "volunteering" for military service, short-sightedness is fomented. This evidence can be seen by the make-up of the military enlisted ranks, which contain the majority of its members from geographic regions of the country that have no manufacturing or productive opportunities left on the market. The depletion of the production of capital goods in the Midwest has directly resulted in more of this part of the country's population being drawn into the armed forces. To escape this lack of opportunity—with the added benefit of "seeing the world" in the numerous countries the US military occupies—men and women from this geographic region are far greater in number in the armed forces (per-capita), than in other areas previously less invested in manufacturing.

More than this though, the actual spending on the nation's large military machine does not reflect the overall deeper effects which have come to be known as the military industrial complex. The production of armament and military machines is the production of consumer goods—at the most, durable consumer goods, but consumer goods nonetheless. The government is interested only in consuming. The expenditures are for present goods. Investment is less a factor. Aircraft and tanks may be assembled here in the United States—with various "private" assembly plants spread throughout the many Congressional districts to keep the political spending going—but capital goods to construct this equipment come from foreigners. And we have already mentioned previously, military expenditures do not lead to prosperity. There is no economic health from war, or "defense" spending. The capital goods sector has suffered directly because of this government-spending burden.

As time goes on, these men and women become more invested in the military way of business and less invested in market experience. Combined with a college education afterwards, it could be years and years before an individual, who enlists from high school, finally experiences life in the private sector of production—if ever. These two categorizes of social forces in American life—the subsidized nature of higher education, and the large military—are delaying any chance that young Americans will have a more prosperous productive life in their older years. As their time-preference changes to more short term thinking, the chance of savings dwindles, and the chance of living pay-check to pay-check is cemented. But this situation has come about precisely because of inflation. Without inflation, other forms of government revenue would be forced to cease in a much faster fashion.

To fund this level of government, the amount of direct taxation on the country would crush the markets instantaneously. More than likely, the revenue would be impossible to collect, as the population would resist. Government borrowing would force interest rates sky high, forcing the legislature to cut the budget. Only by high-jacking the money supply, can the centralized government delay this inevitable termination of events. But in doing so, the economic environment grows all the more precarious. Once the government can no longer expand credit, the crack-up boom will ensue. With enormous swaths of the population jobless, and deeply in debt—with little experience in production to boot—social turmoil will set in.

The Dangers of Centralized Control

As government expenditures increase, at the expense of private property, so too does power ever escalate. The broader aspect of this entire discussion is liberty—which can only be maintained when government is at the very least, restrained and minimized. Marx and Keynes could never "increase freedom" because the root of their respective economic doctrines is merely a call to arms for arbitrary government action.[42] Their followers' screams have justified a slow interventionary march towards centralized power, in a way, by neglecting that freedom can only exist by respecting the natural recognition of private property. In fact, at the core of the lack of domestic American production is simply the growth of centralized American government. Inflation merely provides the optimal means for this power to increase.

Though it has taken centuries, the power of American government over private property has concentrated—albeit slowly—into the hands of a select few. And so it comes as no surprise that many Americans cannot conceive of the notion

---

[42] Though commonly thought of as very different by many economists, the central doctrine espoused by Marx and Keynes is quite similar. As described in an earlier section of this work, to Marx the central "problem" with the market economy was the capitalist, the market entrepreneur who charged "surplus" prices for goods and services. To Keynes, it was the banker's charge of interest rates. To Marx, forcing profits down would raise the workers' income—and for Keynes, forcing interest rates down would "stimulate" economic growth.

that its very own government, once founded by secession from an overbearing regime, can itself become destructive to its own citizenry. The centralization of this power is growing at an exponential rate, and as of now, will only become more "important". The ability to centrally control the money supply is not only the source of inflation, but also enables the much larger symptom of this growth in centralized power. For the purposes of this work, it is fitting to examine the threats an environment like this creates.

When it comes to American government, the Federal is of a different sort. After all, how often can people walk across the street and knock on their congressman's door to ask "Hey, why did you vote yes last week on that house resolution?" Many Americans hardly recognize their representatives' name, yet alone have access to their ear. But as power has increased, it has centralized, and today, the situation has done a complete 180 degree reversal from the local self-government envisioned in 1776. Today, the national government plays a larger role in the individual's life than the local.

Community control offsets the central authority, and the established local and state government associations were meant to serve as a check on the distant power created in 1789. The Federal Government, as formed, was always thought to be "least" important in the individual's life, as this power equates to centralized control. Left unchecked—its only service is to render liberty obsolete. Freedom is inversely proportional to the size of our central government. When centralized government incrementally increases, liberty decreases. If freedom is the root of America, then conversely—the growth in power is the root of its oppression.

Centralized control provides this oppression a venue on a massive scale, so that when this nationalized entity acts, it touches the lives of every American. Alexis de Tocqueville, a renowned Frenchman who visited the United States in the 1830s, was astounded by not just the degree of freedom throughout the various regions of the country, but of the exceptionality of Republic. As can be seen with his writing, he recognized this quite readily and in his famed book *Democracy in America*, Tocqueville wrote of the character of centralized authority, alluding to the absence of it in America at that time:

It profits me but little, after all, that a vigilant authority always protects the tranquility of my pleasures and constantly averts all dangers from my path, without my care or concern, if this same authority is the absolute master of my liberty and my life, and if it so monopolizes movement and life that when it languishes everything languishes around it, that when it sleeps everything must sleep, and that when it dies the state itself must perish.[43]

Unchecked centralized control creates these conditions. The very disposition of centralized authority renders its force supreme, so when it uses said force, its ripples are not of an isolated nature. And just as Jefferson calculated that "the natural progress of things is for liberty to yield while

[43] Tocqueville, Alexis De. *Democracy in America*. Trans. Henry Reeve. Ed. Phillips Bradley. New York: Alfred A. Knopf, 1994. p.92.

government gains ground", so too is there a more specific power movement towards the center—that is, a more consolidated Federal Government. This movement of centralized government began at a creeping pace, but given the passing of time, has continued to escalate.

Red flags about centralized control appeared prior to the adoption of the Constitution, and nearly prevented its ratification. In fact, the fear of an all-powerful central government led some revolutionary-era leaders to take the course of only the simple improvement of the Articles of Confederation, the Constitution's predecessor. Of particular note, this critical era of the Constitutional Convention was marked by the absence of Thomas Jefferson and John Adams, who were both overseas in Paris and London respectively, working towards wider recognition of the new republic. With these men present, history could have taken a different path, for these two were the most prominent "radicals" from the era. Jefferson and Adams, albeit opposed in political parties, were very much critical of centralized power (especially Jefferson). The primary leaders of the movement for British secession, they were literally absent from the whole debate. Jefferson likely would have neutralized James Madison's short-lived alliance with Alexander Hamilton, while Adams—Hamilton's opponent for influence within the Federalist Party, would have likely been weary of his opposition achieving political credit. With Jefferson and Adams present in country during the 1787 discussion, the calls for a new government may not have moved forward.

By this time though, several things had occurred which forced the hand of some of the more cautious leaders to act. One event in 1787 caused a major shift in attitude. Shays' Rebellion began as a small revolt and actually remained that way—but due to a perceived weak and impotent response by the Confederation government—shockwaves of reactionary discourse were perpetuated by established political interest groups.

This period begins the age of the united, yet still sovereign states. Actually, our American ancestors referred to our country as "These States United" or they would say "The United States are"—notice the difference in the last phrase, using the verb "are" and not "is". Despite the granting of new powers to the central government, under the new constitution, the states relinquished these powers in a finite way—mainly under the pretense that resources would be coordinated their common defense. Shay's Rebellions however was merely a scare, creating what Robert Higgs described as a "ratchet effect", whereby government assumes new authority from an assumed crisis.[44]

With the ratification of the constitution, the centralization process had begun. In spite of this, it was still widely understood however that the individual state legislatures would retain nearly all power over affairs not explicitly stated in the new constitution. This viewpoint can be seen quite clearly

---

[44] Higgs, Robert. *Crisis and Leviathan: Critical Episodes in the Growth of American Government.* New York: Oxford UP, 1987. Throughout this work, Robert Higgs reveals that the federal government gained numerous powers during "crisis" situations, justifying a newfound power to solve such "emergencies". Only after the emergency passes, these powers remain intact.

through the writings of James Madison, Alexander Hamilton, and John Jay over and over again throughout the Federalist Papers.

However, for many of the Founders, this assumption of explicit enumerated powers was still not sufficient. The Anti-Federalists pushed hard for a separate Bill of Rights and the 10th Amendment was securely in place:

> ***The powers not delegated to the United States by the Constitution, nor prohibited by it to the States, are reserved to the States respectively, or to the people.***

For some time prior to the American Civil War, the states long served as a careful check on the Federal Government, much more so than the separation of powers in Washington. After all, if a government has its own authority to interpret the extent of its very own powers—i.e. the Supreme Court—how can this power long remain limited?

Though the degradation of the state legislative authority is the subject of a different discussion and cannot be adequately examined here—but the balance of competing entities is gone. Today, the states are merely slaves to the master and the 10th Amendment has little more teeth than a new born pup.

Few though have examined why the states have permitted this to occur, and if historians do examine this question, typically the answer would be rooted in the aftermath of the Civil War—that the War Between the States "settled" the issue of state sovereignty. Notwithstanding, the acceleration of national inflation has also affected the relationship between these entities as well—turning the states into servants of the central authority. For much like the various banks were cartelized under the Federal Reserve system, and hence were permitted to inflate jointly (since they no longer had to compete against one another on the basis of solvency), the states too have ceased competing against the Federal Government (and each other) on the basis of economic freedom. The Federal Government's monetization of debt seeps over into state budgets, which receive hundreds of billions in federal grants and subsidies. Since all state governments receive the benefits from this coordinated budget bloating (and state politicians use this money printing for reelection favors), there is little incentive left for resistance to central control. Inflation then too can not only be seen to undermine economic prosperity, but the very makeup of the American political structure.

The Coming Bust

"Paper money eventually returns to its intrinsic value—zero."

-- Voltaire

This great money-producing scheme cannot last. As Mises wrote, "All booms must come to an end." That the national monetary credit card has continued this long is only a testimony to the amazing zeal of American markets. Though not the focus of our past discussion, we must remember the vigor and wealth of American resources in general—for two great forces have simultaneously been at work. The first we have discussed in detail, the great pressure of monetary inflation, forcing prices ever upward. But the second has also been in play, the force of productivity—which always pushes them down. The private production of goods and services continually increases their supply, causing a natural fall in price. As the division of labor increases in efficiency, the necessary work in which to accomplish different tasks tends to become cheaper. Simply imagine again the two men on an island—one catches the fish and one collects the firewood. Reason dictates that these two men will have a higher standard of living *dividing the labor* via voluntary cooperation, versus both men catching their own fish *and* collecting their own firewood. Living separate and apart, life is typically harder in economic terms. If one understands this, one understands the division of labor—the source of civilization.

In a way, this increase in the ability to produce—the basic definition of economic growth—helps to absorb the expansion of the money supply, and some of the consequential effects from the government printing press. This economic growth can only offset the pace of government printing so long though, and one can see the strangle hold that the price of government debt, as well as printing, has caused on further private production.

For instance, the more resources which are pulled by the government from the private individual, the less and less are available for development. For there are only a finite amount of resources—squandering more and more leads to stagnation. Since this squandering has been done by government via bureaucracy, regulation, taxes, and most significantly, as this analysis has pointed out—inflation, the private producer finds it harder and harder to sustain the amount of government looting. With the stagnation of economic growth and the diminishing "offsetting" force which at essence, helps to indirectly sustain the monetary expansion, inflation will finally prove "victorious". As the liquidation of the American producer continues, the result will be higher and higher prices. This victory of inflation though will likely be short-lived, as markets will always tend to dominate over the long term. However, the nearer-term social consequences of this can be more catastrophic than natural disasters.

"We are in danger of being overwhelmed with irredeemable paper, mere paper, representing not gold nor silver; no sir, representing nothing but broken promises, bad faith, bankrupt corporations, cheated creditors and a ruined people."

-- Daniel Webster

Since the age of the pure fiat dollar, or "soft" money, unchecked inflation has become the status quo worldwide. As mentioned, the war in Vietnam as well as Lyndon Johnson's Great Society, were financed through the Fed's magicians. On the back of this federal printing press, Richard Nixon finally closed the gold window in 1971, signaling the end of the Bretton-Woods agreement. Inevitably, this paper arrangement was bound for doom, as are all government fiat currencies. Leading up to the end of the tie to gold, more and more foreign nations began to demand bullion in exchange for all of the printed dollars which had amassed. Despite all of the "Superpower" pressure the United States commands—it could still not prevent the billions in gold reserves from pouring forth from the Treasury and the Fed. The market was too strong.

Once this final link was severed, inflation only increased, as the value of the dollar was realized to be on a downward trajectory. To reign in this inflationary epidemic, the Fed had no alternative but to raise the overnight funds rate to more than 20%, in a desperate attempt to contract the money supply. But prior to Paul Volcker's high interest rates (beginning under Carter and carrying over into the Reagan years), the Nixon Administration had already worked-out a discrete new arrangement for the post Bretton-Woods era—which merely staved off the coming bust for another day. The major oil producing nations around the globe—especially vital countries such as Saudi Arabia—agreed to sell their oil exports only in terms of dollars. This "demand" from foreign nations for American paper helped to carry the falling dollar past the 1971 entry into the fiat era. When say the United Kingdom purchases oil from Saudi Arabia, British pounds are generally first exchanged for printed dollars—as the transactions run through their respective central banks. These transactions prop up the "petro dollar", created a demand that merely exists because of politics. Of course, individuals and businesses make most of these transactions, but these transactions are by and large facilitated through international central banks. The pyramiding effect of American dollars continues, as those dollars must eventually come back to American borders. Given the appearance that world markets will continually accept American paper, more American paper is printed.[45]

Today, this global resource is still mainly denominated in dollars on the international market, though there does appear to be a growing movement by some nations to move away from this practice. "Currency wars" are the norm now, and this state of affairs grows more heated. Because of the fall from gold, the world's major currencies "float" on the foreign exchange market. Supposedly, this exchange value is determined by the

[45] Of particular note, once these political mechanisms can no longer sustain continued dollar devaluation, more "agreements" from the planners, such as the one reached at Bretton-Woods, may still be in store down the road. If these monetary agreements take shape without the roots of honest money, they will fail as well.

market forces of supply and demand. But take away the government coercion, and there is no demand for paper money. Additionally, we can easily debunk this flawed concept that somehow floating currencies best provide "fair trade". Floating currencies essentially serve as trading barriers, as individual governments are convinced that a more devalued currency, relative to its foreign competition, is somehow the most beneficial to economic growth. Printing more money is better for growth! Absurd! But this is exactly what the Federal Reserve is chasing right now, through "quantitative easing". Think back to the analogy about the 50 states in the American union—if each state decided to issue its own currency and permit it to "float", trade would be not only chaotic, but paralyzed. Now imagine if every household in America decided to issue its own floating paper currency, and you realize the fallacy of the government-fiat exchange system.

In the short term, export sales appear more robust with an ever devaluing US dollar. But all that is transpired is the further debasement of the dollar, redistributing wealth to the holders of these new dollars. The American producer is fooled that he is receiving more resources for his sales since all of his raw materials are denominated in dollars, he at first cannot distinguish the harm. But in the long run, his prices go up, and his real profits are diminished. For the same numeric sell price, the exporter loses more resources, all because of the "benefits of the devalued dollar". Of course, importers realize the harm more quickly, as their raw material prices rise with the falling dollar—the vendors to the American importer denominating their own sales on the foreign exchange market. But in general, the newly printed dollars originate with the American market—the US financial industry. This "privilege" provides American markets with "first come" dibs when utilizing the counterfeit against foreign goods. The banking sector becomes more bloated, and the domestic producer is squeezed thin. The national credit card gets fatter.

The day of reckoning is nearing. The national government's debt stands at more than 16 trillion dollars, virtually equaling the country's total gross domestic product. This figure does not represent future liabilities or other obligations that have been publicly pledged. Budget deficits are over 1 trillion, and as of now, appear to remain that way for the foreseeable future. Interest rates have been held at near zero percent for over 3 years, and are also pledged to be held this low for the years to come. Of this surging national debt, over 5 trillion is held by foreign governments, with the annual trade deficit projected to surge beyond 600 billion (the trade deficit with China alone is nearly half of this figure, now over 250 billion). These numbers, staggering as they are, have become meaningless to government officials—especially the central bank, its board members adamantly insisting there is no connection between the insanity of printing money and the destruction of American productivity. The last Federal "Stimulus" bill of nearly one trillion borrowed dollars was nothing compared to the amount of money which has been created from government whim. This monetary policy has simply prolonged economic recovery, while widening fiscal insolvency. To top all this off, the economy is running right now with a meager average savings rate. Savings is a thing of the past.

American foreign affairs grow increasingly heated. Talk of war grows steady. Political rhetoric abounds about the modern war on terror, and still, the public is hard pressed to realize the connection between the shrinking dollar, the rising price of oil, the instability that comes with American intervention overseas, and the enormous amounts of wealth needed to sustain the United States warfare state.

There is no such thing as capitalism without capital, or long term prosperity without savings, irrespective of how much money is printed. It is critical to realize that this fiscal nightmare can only exist with the government's monopoly of the mint. Getting a handle now will take some amount of pain, but will stave off misery. After enough printing—and as soon as the first foreign nation "dumps" its dollar reserves—those dollars will come roaring home. Then it will be too late. If policy does not change course, the end game will eventually become public default, in an overt manner—or hyperinflation. Neither is inevitable, but if current American policy stays the given course, history and economics tells us the outcome.

References

Bagus, Philipp. *The Tragedy of the Euro*. Auburn, Ala.: Ludwig Von Mises, 2010.

Bastiat, Claude Frederic. *The Bastiat Collection*. Second ed. Auburn, Alabama: Ludwig Von Mises Institute, 2011.

Bastiat, Frederic. *The Law*. Auburn, Ala: Ludwig Von Mises Institute, 2007.

De Soto, Jesus Huerta. *Money, Bank Credit, and Economic Cycles*. Trans. Melinda A. Stroup. Second ed. Auburn, Alabama: Ludwig Von Mises Institute, 2009.

Denson, John V. *The Costs of War: America's Pyrrhic Victories*. New Brunswick, N.J., U.S.A.: Transaction, 1999.

Erlichman, Howard J. *Conquest, Tribute, and Trade: The Quest for Precious Metals and the Birth of Globalization*. Amherst, NY: Prometheus, 2010.

Fergusson, Adam. *When Money Dies: The Nightmare of Deficit Spending, Devaluation, and Hyperinflation in Weimar Germany*. New York: Public Affairs, 2010.

French, Douglas Edward. *Early Speculative Bubbles and Increase in the Supply of Money.* Auburn, Ala.: Ludwig Von Mises Institute, 2009.

Gibbon, Edward. *The Decline and Fall of the Roman Empire.* Ed. Hans-Friedrich .. Mueller. New York: Modern Library, 2003.

Hayek, Friedrich A. *Prices and Production and Other Works: F. A. Hayek on Money, the Business Cycle, and the Gold Standard.* Ed. Joseph Salerno. Auburn, Alabama: Ludwig Von Mises Institute, 2008.

Hayek, Friedrich A. Von. *The Road to Serfdom: Text and Documents.* Ed. Bruce Caldwell. Vol. II. Chicago: University of Chicago, 2007.

Hazlitt, Henry. *Economics in One Lesson.* New York: Arlington House, 1979.

Hazlitt, Henry. *The Inflation Crisis, and How to Resolve It.* New Rochelle, NY: Arlington House, 1978.

Herring, George C. *America's Longest War: The United States and Vietnam, 1950-1975.* Fourth ed. New York: McGraw-Hill, 2002.

Higgs, Robert. *Crisis and Leviathan: Critical Episodes in the Growth of American Government.* New York: Oxford UP, 1987.

Hoppe, Hans-Hermann. *Democracy--The God That Failed: The Economics and Politics of Monarchy, Democracy and Natural Order.* New Brunswick, NJ: Transaction, 2001.

Jouvenel, Bertrand De. *On Power: The Natural History of Its Growth.* Indianapolis: Liberty Fund, 1993.

Kelly, Kel. "The China Bust: Tic Toc." *Ludwig Von Mises Institute.* Mises Institute, 10 Oct. 2011. Web. <http://mises.org/daily/5701>.

Keynes, John Maynard. *A Treatise on Money.* New York: Harcourt, Brace and Company, 1930.

Keynes, John Maynard. *The General Theory of Employment, Interest and Money.* New York: Harcourt, 1964.

Marx, Karl, and Friedrich Engels. *The Communist Manifesto and Other Writings.* Comp. Martin Puchner. New York: Barnes & Noble, 2005.

Mises, Ludwig Von. *Human Action: A Treatise on Economics.* Auburn, Ala: Ludwig Von Mises Institute, 2008.

Mises, Ludwig Von. *Nation, State and Economy: Contributions to the Politics and History of Our Time.* Leland B. Yeager, trans. New York: New York University Press, 1983.

Mises, Ludwig Von. *Socialism: An Economic and Sociological Analysis.* New Haven: Yale UP, 1951.

Mises, Ludwig Von. *The Causes of the Economic Crisis: And Other Essays before and after the Great Depression.* Ed. Percy L. Greaves. Auburn, Ala.: Ludwig Von Mises Institute, 2006.

Mises, Ludwig Von. *The Theory of Money and Credit.* New Haven: Yale UP, 1953.

Paine, Thomas. *Common Sense, Rights of Man, and Other Essential Writings of Thomas Paine.* New York: Signet Classic, 2003.

Peden, Joseph. "Inflation and the Fall of the Roman Empire", *LewRockwell*.com. 18 Aug. 2009. Web. < http://www.lewrockwell.com/orig10/peden1.1.1.html>.

Phillips, Chester Arthur, Thomas Francis McManus, and Richard Ward Nelson. *Banking and the Business Cycle; a Study of the Great Depression in the United States.* New York: Macmillan, 1937.

Rothbard, Murray. *A History of Money and Banking in the United States: The Colonial Era to World War II.* Auburn, Ala.: Ludwig Von Mises Institute, 2005.

Rothbard, Murray. *America's Great Depression.* Princeton, NJ: Van Nostrand, 1963.

Rothbard, Murray. *Man, Economy, and State with Power and Market.* Second ed. Auburn, Alabama: Ludwig Von Mises Institute, 2009.

Rothbard, Murray Newton. *What Has Government Done to Our Money?: And, The Case for a 100 Percent Gold Dollar.* Fifth ed. Auburn, Ala.: Ludwig Von Mises Institute, 2005.

Smith, Adam. *The Wealth of Nations.* Ed. Edwin Cannan. New York: Modern Library, 1994.

Tocqueville, Alexis De. *Democracy in America.* Trans. Henry

Reeve. Ed. Phillips Bradley. New York: Alfred A. Knopf, 1994.

Wapshott, Nicholas. *Keynes Hayek: The Clash That Defined Modern Economics.* New York: W.W. Norton & Company, 2011.

Printed in Dunstable, United Kingdom

91342768R00127